"IRIE" is one of the many colorful words from Jamaica's native language called patois. It is a common greeting on the island, a way of saying "everything is okay."

The title *Sugar and Spice and Everything Irie* is our way of saying you will enjoy the recipes in this book; some are sweet, some are savory — and all are authentic. These recipes are for anyone who has the desire to explore the beauty of Jamaica and its culture through its cuisine.

SUGAR AND SPICE
&
EVERYTHING IRIE

Savoring Jamaica's Flavors

VEDA NUGENT AND MARRETT GREEN

Callawind
Publications Inc.

Sugar and Spice and Everything Irie: Savoring Jamaica's Flavors

Copyright © 2001 by Veda Nugent and Marrett Green

All rights reserved. The use of any part of this publication, reproduced, transmitted in any form or by any means, electronic, mechanical, recorded or otherwise, or stored in a retrieval system, without the prior consent of the publisher is an infringement of the copyright law.

CATALOGUING IN PUBLICATION DATA
Nugent, Veda.
   Sugar and spice & everything irie : savoring Jamaica's flavors

Includes index.
ISBN 1-896511-16-3

   1. Cookery, Jamaican. I. Green, Marrett, 1967– II. Title.

TX716.J27N84 2001   641.597292   C2001-901708-1

Copy editing by Shaun Oakey. Design by Marcy Claman. Indexing by Christine Jacobs.
Cover photos: Jamaican Street Vendor courtesy of Jamaica Tourist Board. Jamaican Cuisine (Ocho Rios) and Rafting on the Martha Brae, Kevin Garrett.

10 9 8 7 6 5 4 3 2 1

Printed in Canada.
All product/brand names are trademarks or registered trademarks of their respective trademark holders.

Published by Callawind Publications Inc.
   3539 St. Charles Boulevard, Suite 179, Kirkland, Quebec, Canada H9H 3C4
   2083 Hempstead Turnpike, PMB 355, East Meadow, New York, USA 11554-1711
   E-mail: info@callawind.com   http://www.callawind.com

DISCLAIMER AND LIMITS OF LIABILITY
This book is sold as is, without warranty of any kind, either express or implied, respecting the contents of this book, including but not limited to implied warranties for the book's quality, performance, merchantability, or fitness for any particular purpose. Neither the authors nor Callawind Publications Inc. or its dealers or distributors shall be liable to the purchaser or any other person or entity with respect to any liability, loss, or damage caused or alleged to be caused directly or indirectly by the use of this book.

"For health and strength and daily
food we praise Thy Name, O Lord."

~~~~~~

ACKNOWLEDGMENTS

I cannot begin to count the number of friends and restaurant customers who have encouraged me to publish my recipes. There are far too many for me to thank individually. My deepest thanks go out to all of you for your sincerity and persistence.

I give special thanks to my daughters, Gardiea and Natasha, my son-in-law, Fred, and to my son, Marrett, the co-author of this book.

Foremost credit for this book, however, goes to my mother, Miss Ruby, the strongest person I know. She taught me life values of patience and love and the importance of cooking with heart. Thanks, Mom.

— VEDA NUGENT

CONTENTS

~~~~~~~~~~~~~~~~~~~~~~~~~~~~~~~~~~~~

5. VEGETABLES

6. SIDE DISHES

7. BEVERAGES

7. BEVERAGES (CONTINUED)

8. DESSERTS

9. SAUCES & DIPS

INTRODUCTION

~~~~~~

I WAS BORN TO COOK. I WAS THE ONLY GIRL IN A FAMILY OF TWELVE CHILDREN LIVING IN THE COUNTRYSIDE OF FLINT RIVER, JAMAICA, AND SO THERE WAS LITTLE DISCUSSION ABOUT WHERE I WAS MOST NEEDED; I VIRTUALLY GREW UP IN OUTDOOR KITCHENS AND I COULD NOT HAVE ASKED FOR A BETTER INTRODUCTION TO COOKING.

When I was ten, I would occasionally help my mother prepare meals outside for the maintenance men on the island's railway line. Today, the line is no longer in use, but back then it carried both commuters and freight. It ran through several parishes on the west side of the island, connecting Kingston, the capital, to Port Antonio on the coast. The main freight was bananas being carried from farms to Port Antonio, from where they were shipped to England and the United States. The return trains were always filled with hagglers carrying their produce to Coronation Market in Kingston.

My mother's railway kitchen was one canvas tent, where the men would eat, and an outdoor wood fire, where she would cook. The fire was circled with stones on which sat three pieces of discarded railway track; each track piece was about a foot long. Her cast-iron dutchies (pots) would sit on top. Sometimes my mother had as many as six dutchies cooking at once.

Although I was ready for any task, my contribution to the railway kitchen was mainly unpacking supplies and fetching pots. There was very little a ten-year-old child could do, yet my mother did have a way of making me feel important. It was then that I learned the significance of preparing hearty meals. Dining etiquette and the delicate points of cuisine presentation were not essential when feeding twelve hungry men outdoors. My discipline in those finer qualities did not come until much later, when I was about sixteen and attending Miss Mays' Cooking Classes. Miss Mays' was one of the island's most promising cooking schools, teaching the art of Jamaican cuisine.

It was at Miss Mays' that I began noticing my island's diverse culture and its influence on the island cuisine. Many of Jamaica's natives are of African descent; others are East Indian, Spanish, Chinese, European . . . hence the island's national motto: Out of Many, One People.

Jamaica's original inhabitants were Arawaks, who arrived in tree-trunk canoes from South America nearly 2,500 years ago. They named the island Xaymaca, which means "land of wood and water." One of their legacies to traditional Jamaican dishes is called spicy fried fish, and it's still a popular meal today. The Arawaks were also one of the first to jerk meats, a method of preserving meat without refrigeration. Little did they know that their practical technique would evolve into one of the more popular styles of Jamaican cooking. Today, jerk pork, jerk chicken, and jerk fish are highlights of Jamaican cuisine.

From 1494, when Christopher Columbus and the Spaniards landed on the island's shores and founded Spanish Town, to the 1700s, when buccaneers (their name originates from "bukan," referring to the way they would cook and dry their meat) used Jamaica as a sea port, many different cultures have been adding to the island's cooking pot.

The recipes in this book emerge from a diverse culture, now centuries old, and they tell the story of an island and its people through its native cooking. Enjoy!

APPETIZERS & SNACKS

~~~~~~

"ONE, ONE COCO FUL BASKIT"

Appreciate every little thing
you receive in life.

JERK PORK AND JERK CHICKEN PÂTÉ

THIS PÂTÉ CAN ALSO BE PREPARED USING THE SAME AMOUNT OF BONELESS JERK CHICKEN (PAGE 70) AS JERK PORK.

Preparation and cooking time: 10 to 15 minutes   **Yield: 8–10 servings**

1 pound / 500 g boneless jerk pork (page 67)
1 small onion, chopped (about ¼ cup / 60 mL)
½ teaspoon / 2 mL finely chopped hot pepper

1 teaspoon / 5 mL Worcestershire sauce
¼ cup / 60 mL rum
½ teaspoon / 2 mL ground ginger

PURÉE the jerk pork in a blender or food processor. Add the onion, hot pepper, and Worcestershire sauce; blend to combine. Scoop the mixture into an oven-to-table container.

POUR the rum into a small saucepan and carefully set it afire. Let the rum burn for 10 seconds, then carefully pour it over the jerk pork mixture. Very carefully, stir the rum through the mixture once and allow the flames to extinguish. Mix in the ginger.

SERVE on your favorite crackers, coconut chips (page 96), or roti (page 84).

JAMAICAN CHICKEN PATTIES

I CAME UP WITH THIS PATTY WHEN PEOPLE WERE TURNING AWAY FROM BEEF FOR ONE REASON OR THE OTHER. I WOULD NEVER HAVE GUESSED THAT CATERING TO THIS DIETARY TREND WOULD HAVE PRODUCED SUCH A DELIGHTFUL AND TASTY TREAT.

Preparation and cooking time: 1 to 1½ hours   **Yield: 15–20 patties**

1 cup / 250 mL dry bread crumbs
2 cups / 500 mL water
2 tablespoons / 25 mL vegetable oil
1 large onion, finely chopped (about ½ cup / 125 mL)

5 green onions, chopped (about 1 cup / 250 mL)
4 cloves garlic, finely chopped
   (about 2 tablespoons / 25 mL)
½ Scotch bonnet pepper, finely chopped
   (about 1 teaspoon / 5 mL)

1 pound / 500 g skinless, boneless chicken, washed and
   finely chopped
2 teaspoons / 10 mL thyme leaves
2 teaspoons / 10 mL curry powder

1 teaspoon / 5 mL salt
1 teaspoon / 5 mL black pepper
15–20 patty shells (page 15)

STIR the bread crumbs and water together and set aside.

HEAT the oil in a medium saucepan over medium-high heat. Sauté the onion, green onions, garlic, and Scotch bonnet pepper until the vegetables are soft. Reduce the heat to medium and add the chicken, thyme, curry powder, salt, and black pepper. Sauté for 10 to 15 minutes or until the chicken is cooked through, stirring frequently to ensure the filling does not stick to the bottom of the pan. Stir in the bread crumbs and simmer for 5 to 10 minutes or until the filling has the consistency of soft mashed potatoes. Remove from the heat and set aside to cool.

PREHEAT the oven to 350°F / 180°C. Lightly grease a baking sheet.

PUT 2 heaping tablespoons / 25 mL of filling in the center of each patty shell. Fold the shell in half to create a half-moon shape and with a fork press along the edges to seal, pressing in about ½ inch / 1 cm from the edge.

PLACE the patties on the baking sheet and bake for 20 to 25 minutes or until golden brown. Serve hot.

JAMAICAN BEEF PATTIES

THE BEEF PATTY IS THE TRADITIONAL SNACK OF THE ISLAND. PATTIES CAN BE FOUND IN EVERY CORNER OF JAMAICA. THE PATTIES IN THIS COOKBOOK HAVE BEEN PERFECTED OVER NEARLY TWO DECADES AS I'VE MADE THEM FOR MY RESTAURANT CUSTOMERS AND FAMILY. A WARNING TO YOU: YOUR FRIENDS AND FAMILY WILL NOT LET YOU GET AWAY WITH MAKING THIS RECIPE ONLY ONCE.

Preparation and cooking time: 1 to 1½ hours   Yield: 15–20 patties

1 cup / 250 mL dry bread crumbs
2 cups / 500 mL water
2 tablespoons / 25 mL vegetable oil
1 large onion, finely chopped (about ½ cup / 125 mL)
5 green onions, finely chopped (about 1 cup / 250 mL)
4 cloves garlic, finely chopped (about 2 tablespoons / 25 mL)
½ Scotch bonnet pepper, finely chopped (about 1 teaspoon / 5 mL)

1 pound / 500 g lean ground beef
2 teaspoons / 10 mL thyme leaves
2 teaspoons / 10 mL curry powder
1 teaspoon / 5 mL salt
1 teaspoon / 5 mL black pepper
15–20 patty shells (page 15)

STIR the bread crumbs and water together and set aside.

Heat the oil in a medium saucepan over medium-high heat. Sauté the onion, green onions, garlic, and Scotch bonnet pepper until the vegetables are soft. Reduce heat to medium and add the beef, thyme, curry powder, salt, and black pepper. Sauté until the beef is no longer pink, stirring frequently to ensure the filling does not stick to the bottom of the pan. Stir in the bread crumbs and simmer for 5 to 10 minutes or until the filling has the consistency of creamy mashed potatoes. Remove from the heat and set aside to cool.

PREHEAT the oven to 350°F / 180°C. Lightly grease a baking sheet.

PUT 2 heaping tablespoons / 25 mL of filling in the center of each patty shell. Fold the shell in half to create a half-moon shape and with a fork press along the edges to seal, pressing in about ½ inch / 1 cm from the edge.

PLACE the patties on the baking sheet and bake for 20 to 25 minutes or until golden brown. Serve hot.

JAMAICAN BEEF PATTIES (CONTINUED)

Yield: 15–20 patty shells

Patty Shells

4 cups / 1 L all-purpose flour
1 teaspoon / 5 mL salt
1½ cups / 375 mL shortening

1 egg
1 tablespoon / 15 mL vinegar

Mix the flour and salt in a large bowl. Cut in the shortening with a knife, then use your hands or a pastry blender to rub the shortening into the flour until the mixture is crumbly.

In a measuring cup, beat the egg. Add the vinegar and enough water to make 1 cup / 250 mL. Stir. Make a well in the center of the flour mixture and add ½ cup / 125 mL of the egg mixture. Stir with a fork until the mixture forms a dough, adding more liquid a tablespoon / 15 mL at a time if necessary. Roll the dough into a ball, flatten it into a disk, wrap it in a clean kitchen cloth, and refrigerate it for 1 hour.

Divide the dough into 15 to 20 equal portions, and roll each portion into a ball. On a floured surface roll each ball to the size of a salad plate (about 6 inches / 15 cm in diameter). Fill and bake according to your recipe.

JAMAICAN VEGETABLE PATTIES

WHILE OPERATING ONE OF OUR RESTAURANTS IN OTTAWA, I CREATED THIS PATTY FOR OUR VEGETARIAN CUSTOMERS. THESE PATTIES ARE SPICY AND DELICIOUS.

Preparation and cooking time: 1 to 1½ hours

Yield: 15–20 patties

1 cup / 250 mL dry bread crumbs
2 cups / 500 mL water
2 tablespoons / 25 mL vegetable oil
1 large onion, finely chopped (about ½ cup / 375 mL)
5 green onions, chopped (about 1 cup / 250 mL)
4 cloves garlic, finely chopped
  (about 2 tablespoons / 25 mL)
½ Scotch bonnet pepper, finely chopped
  (about 1 teaspoon / 5 mL)

4 cups / 1 L frozen mixed vegetables
2 teaspoons / 10 mL thyme leaves
2 teaspoons / 10 mL curry powder
1 teaspoon / 15 mL salt
1 teaspoon / 15 mL black pepper
15–20 patty shells (page 15)

STIR the bread crumbs and water together and set aside.

HEAT the oil in a medium saucepan over medium-high heat. Sauté the onion, green onions, garlic, and Scotch bonnet pepper until soft. Reduce heat to medium and add the vegetables, thyme, curry powder, salt, and black pepper. Sauté the vegetables until they are cooked yet crispy, stirring frequently to ensure the filling does not stick to the bottom of the pan. Stir in the bread crumbs and simmer for 5 to 10 minutes or until the filling has the consistency of soft mashed potatoes. Remove from the heat and set aside to cool.

PREHEAT the oven to 350°F / 180°C. Lightly grease a baking sheet.

PUT 2 heaping tablespoons / 25 mL of filling in the center of each patty shell. Fold the shell in half to create a half-moon shape and with a fork press along the edges to seal, pressing in about ½ inch / 1 cm from the edge.

PLACE the patties on the baking sheet and bake for 20 to 25 minutes or until golden brown. Serve hot.

JAMAICAN SALTED CODFISH PATTIES

IT WAS MY LOVE FOR SALTFISH THAT INSPIRED ME TO CREATE THIS TASTY TREAT FOR MYSELF. BUT AFTER SHARING IT WITH FAMILY, FRIENDS, AND CUSTOMERS, THE DEMAND BECAME SO GREAT, IT WAS ADDED TO OUR RESTAURANT MENU.

Preparation and cooking time: 2 hours   Yield: 15–20 patties

1 cup / 250 mL dry bread crumbs
2 cups / 500 mL water
2 tablespoons / 25 mL vegetable oil
1 large onion, finely chopped (about ½ cup / 125 mL)
5 green onions, chopped (about 1 cup / 250 mL)
4 cloves garlic, finely chopped
   (about 2 tablespoons / 25 mL)
½ Scotch bonnet pepper, finely chopped
   (about 1 teaspoon / 5 mL)

3 cups / 750 mL shredded, desalted, and deboned
   salted codfish*
2 teaspoons / 10 mL thyme leaves
2 teaspoons / 10 mL curry powder
1 teaspoon / 5 mL salt
1 teaspoon / 5 mL black pepper
15–20 patty shells (page 15)

*For desalting codfish, see page 38.

STIR the bread crumbs and water together and set aside.

HEAT the oil in a medium saucepan over medium-high heat. Sauté the onion, green onions, garlic, and Scotch bonnet pepper until the vegetables are soft. Reduce heat to medium and add the fish, thyme, curry powder, salt, and black pepper. Sauté for 3 to 5 minutes or until the fish is heated through, stirring frequently to ensure the filling does not stick to the bottom of the pan. Stir in the bread crumbs and simmer for 5 to 10 minutes or until the filling has the consistency of soft mashed potatoes. Remove from the heat and set aside to cool.

PREHEAT the oven to 350°F / 180°C. Lightly grease a baking sheet.

PUT 2 heaping tablespoons / 25 mL of filling in the center of each patty shell. Fold the shell in half to create a half-moon shape and with a fork press along the edges to seal, pressing in about ½ inch / 1 cm from the edge.

PLACE the patties on the baking sheet and bake for 20 to 25 minutes or until golden brown. Serve hot.

SALTED CODFISH FRITTERS

THIS IS ONE OF JAMAICA'S STAPLE TREATS. THEY ARE MADE IN EVERY HOME AND CAN BE HAD AT ALMOST EVERY SCHOOL AT RECESS AND LUNCHTIME. THERE MIGHT BE VARIATIONS IN TEXTURE — SOME PEOPLE LIKE THEM LIGHT AND FLUFFY, SOME ADD COLOR WITH CURRY OR KETCHUP, AND SOME LIKE THIS PARTICULAR RECIPE, WHICH WAS PASSED ON TO ME BY MY MOTHER.

Preparation and cooking time: 30 minutes   Yield: 3–4 servings

If you use the optional egg in this recipe, the fritters will be softer and fluffier. Without the egg, you'll get a firmer result.

1 cup / 250 mL all-purpose flour
¾ cup / 175 mL water
1 egg (optional)
½ pound / 250 g salted codfish, desalted, deboned, cooked, and minced*
3 green onions, finely chopped (about ¾ cup / 175 mL)

½ small tomato, diced (about ¼ cup / 60 mL)
1 teaspoon / 5 mL thyme leaves
½ teaspoon / 2 mL finely chopped hot pepper
½ teaspoon / 2 mL black pepper
¼ teaspoon / 1 mL salt (optional)
2 cups / 500 mL vegetable oil

*For desalting codfish, see page 38.

IN a medium bowl, combine the flour, water, and egg. Stir together well. Add the salted codfish, green onions, tomato, thyme, hot pepper, black pepper, and salt. Mix thoroughly. The consistency should be a little thinner than pancake batter; add a little more water if necessary.

IN a large, deep skillet over medium heat, heat the oil until hot but not smoking. Working in batches if necessary, drop the batter by the tablespoonful into the oil and fry the fritters for 2 to 3 minutes or until golden brown on the bottom. Turn them and fry the other side until golden brown, about 2 to 3 minutes.

DRAIN the fritters on paper towels and serve hot.

SOUPS
~~~~~~~~

"TOO MUCH RATA NEVA DIG GOOD OLE"

Too many cooks spoil the soup.

JAMAICAN OXTAIL SOUP 1

TRADITIONALLY, OXTAIL IS COOKED IN A STEW WITH LIMA BEANS, BUT I FEEL THAT IT IS FAR TOO TASTY A CUT OF MEAT TO LIMIT TO ONE DISH. WHEN PREPARED PROPERLY, OXTAIL WILL ABSORB ALL THE FLAVORS OF THE SPICES IT'S COOKED IN.

Preparation and cooking time: 2 to 3 hours

Yield: 5–8 servings

5½ quarts / 5.5 L water
3 pounds / 1.5 kg oxtail, cut at the joints by your butcher
1 large onion, peeled
6 cloves garlic, chopped (about 3 tablespoons / 45 mL)
1 tablespoon / 15 mL salt
1 (1-pound / 500-g) pumpkin, peeled and diced (about 4 cups / 1 L)
2 small turnips, sliced (about 2 cups / 500 mL)
1 large carrot, chopped (about 1 cup / 250 mL)
2 chochos, peeled and sliced
½ pound / 250 g yellow yam, cut into large cubes

2 potatoes, quartered
1 coco, cut in half
Dough for Boiled Dumplings (page 86)
5 green onions, chopped (about 1 cup / 250 mL)
1 Scotch bonnet pepper
1 (1-ounce / 28-g) packet beef noodle soup mix
2 tablespoons / 25 mL whole pimento seeds (allspice)
1 tablespoon / 15 mL butter
1 teaspoon / 5 mL thyme leaves or 2 sprigs of fresh thyme
½ teaspoon / 2 mL black pepper

IN a stockpot, bring the water to a rolling boil. Wash the oxtail thoroughly in cold water. Add the oxtail, onion, garlic, and salt to the boiling water. Cover the pot and boil, occasionally skimming the scum as it forms on the surface, usually in the first 10 minutes of boiling. Reduce the heat to medium and simmer for 45 minutes or until the oxtail is almost tender.

ADD the pumpkin, turnips, and carrot; simmer for 15 minutes.

DISCARD the onion. Add the chochos, yellow yams, potatoes, and coco. Simmer for 5 minutes, stirring frequently to prevent the ingredients sticking to the bottom of the pot.

ADD the dumplings and bring the soup to a rolling boil; boil for 5 minutes. Reduce the heat to medium and simmer, stirring occasionally, for another 15 to 20 minutes or just until the ingredients are tender. Don't overcook.

ADD the green onions, Scotch bonnet pepper, beef soup mix, pimento seeds, butter, thyme, and black pepper; stir well. Cover and simmer for 5 more minutes.

DISCARD the Scotch bonnet pepper (don't burst the pepper) and pimento seeds. Serve hot.

JAMAICAN OXTAIL SOUP II

I CREATED THIS RECIPE SOON AFTER MY FAMILY ARRIVED IN CANADA IN THE EARLY 1970s, WHEN WE WERE CRAVING OUR FAVORITE JAMAICAN DISHES. BECAUSE WE COULDN'T FIND SOME OF THE TRADITIONAL INGREDIENTS, I DECIDED TO PREPARE THE SOUP WITH SLIGHT VARIATIONS — FLOURED AND SEASONED OXTAIL AND MINUS THE "EXOTIC" COCO AND CHOCHO.

Preparation and cooking time: 2 to 3 hours

Yield: 5–8 servings

3 pounds / 1.5 kg oxtail, cut at the joints by your butcher
1 teaspoon / 5 mL salt
½ teaspoon / 2 mL black pepper
All-purpose flour to coat oxtail
2 tablespoons / 25 mL butter
1 large onion, chopped (about 1½ cups / 375 mL)
4 cloves garlic, chopped (about 2 tablespoons / 25 mL)
6 cups / 1.5 L beef stock

1 tablespoon / 15 mL soy sauce
2 stalks celery, chopped (about 2 cups / 500 mL)
1 large carrot, chopped (about 1 cup / 250 mL)
1 small turnip, chopped (about 1 cup / 250 mL)
1 Scotch bonnet pepper (optional)
¼ teaspoon / 1 mL cayenne pepper
2 teaspoons / 10 mL Worcestershire sauce

WASH the oxtail and sprinkle with the salt and black pepper. Lightly coat the oxtail with the flour and shake off any excess. In a large skillet over medium heat, melt the butter. Add the oxtail and brown it on all sides.

TRANSFER the oxtail and its drippings to a stockpot. Add the onion, garlic, stock, and soy sauce. Cover the pot and bring to a simmer over medium-low heat. Simmer until the oxtail is tender, 1½ to 2 hours.

REMOVE the oxtail from the pot and cut the meat from the bones. Set the meat aside.

To the liquid, add the celery, carrot, turnip, whole Scotch bonnet pepper, and cayenne. Simmer, covered, over medium-low heat, for 10 to 15 minutes or until the vegetables are tender.

DISCARD the Scotch bonnet pepper (don't burst the pepper). Add the meat and Worcestershire sauce; simmer until the meat is heated through. Serve hot.

FiSH TEA (SOUP)

MANY JAMAICAN PARENTS STRAIN FISH TEA THROUGH A CHEESECLOTH AND FEED IT TO THEIR INFANTS AND TODDLERS, TO PROVIDE THE INDISPUTABLE NUTRITIONAL VALUE OF FISH AT THE EARLIEST AGE POSSIBLE.

Preparation and cooking time: 1 hour

Yield: 4–5 servings

8 cups / 2 L water
1 lime
2 pounds / 1 kg fish (or 4 large fish heads, cleaned)
4 cloves garlic, chopped (about 2 tablespoons / 25 mL)
¼ teaspoon / 1 mL salt
2 green bananas, finely chopped (about 2 cups / 500 mL)
1 potato, peeled and finely chopped
   (about 1 cup / 250 mL)
1 chocho, peeled and finely chopped
   (about 1 cup / 250 mL)

1 carrot, peeled and finely chopped
   (about ⅔ cup / 150 mL)
3 green onions, chopped (about ¾ cup / 175 mL)
1 Scotch bonnet pepper
1 (1-ounce / 28-g) packet chicken noodle soup mix
½ teaspoon / 2 mL dried thyme or 1 sprig of fresh thyme
1 tablespoon / 15 mL butter

IN a stockpot, bring the water to a rolling boil. Squeeze the lime juice over the fish; let it sit for a couple of minutes and then rinse with cold water. Add the fish, garlic, and salt to the boiling water. Boil, skimming the scum as it forms on the surface, usually in the first 10 minutes of boiling. Reduce the heat to medium, cover, and simmer for about 30 minutes. Let the soup cool.

STRAIN the soup through a fine sieve and return the broth to the pot, reserving the fish. (If you are using fish heads, discard the heads.) Add the green bananas, potato, chocho, and carrot. Cover the pot and cook over medium-low heat for 10 to 15 minutes or until the vegetables begin to get tender.

MEANWHILE, debone the fish. Add the fish, green onions, Scotch bonnet pepper, chicken soup mix, and thyme to the soup. Reduce heat to low and simmer for 10 to 15 minutes or until the fish is heated through.

DISCARD the Scotch bonnet pepper (don't burst it) and stir in the butter. Serve hot.

JAMAICAN BEEF SOUP

IN JAMAICA, THIS SOUP IS A STAPLE, SERVED AS A COMPLETE MEAL IN MANY HOMES EVERY SATURDAY EVENING.

Preparation and cooking time: 1½ to 2 hours

Yield: 6–8 servings

5 quarts / 5 L water
2 pounds / 1 kg stewing beef
1 large onion, peeled
6 cloves garlic, chopped (about 3 tablespoons / 45 mL)
1 teaspoon / 5 mL salt
1 (1-pound / 500-g) pumpkin, peeled and diced (about 4 cups / 1 L)
1 cup / 250 mL sliced carrots
2 small turnips, diced (about 2 cups / 500 mL)
2 chochos, peeled and sliced
1 pound / 500 g yellow yams, cut in chunks

2 medium potatoes, quartered
1 coco, cut in half
Dough for Boiled Dumplings (page 86)
4 green onions, chopped (about 1 cup / 250 mL)
2 sprigs of fresh thyme (or 1 teaspoon / 5 mL dried thyme)
1 Scotch bonnet pepper
2 ounces / 50 g vermicelli noodles
1 (1-ounce / 28-g) packet beef noodle soup mix
1 tablespoon / 15 mL butter

IN a stockpot, bring the water to a rolling boil. Wash the beef thoroughly in cold water. Carefully add the beef, onion, garlic, and salt. Boil, skimming the scum as it forms on the surface, usually in the first 10 minutes of boiling. Cover the pot and lower the heat to medium-low. Simmer for 45 to 60 minutes or until the beef is partially tender.

DISCARD the onion. Add the pumpkin, carrots, turnips, and chochos. Simmer for 10 to 15 minutes. Add the yellow yams, potatoes, coco, and dumplings. Cover the pot and bring the soup to a rapid boil; boil for 3 minutes. Reduce the heat to low and simmer until all vegetables are tender. Don't overcook.

ADD the green onions, thyme, Scotch bonnet pepper, vermicelli, beef soup mix, and butter. Cover the pot and simmer for another 5 to 10 minutes or until noodles are tender.

DISCARD the Scotch bonnet pepper (don't burst it) and thyme sprigs. Serve hot.

CREAM OF CALLALOO SOUP WITH OKRA

THIS RECIPE IS MOST DEAR TO ME. ITS AROMA TAKES ME RIGHT BACK TO MY MOTHER'S KITCHEN, WHERE I HAVE FOND CHILDHOOD MEMORIES OF WATCHING HER PREPARE THIS SOUP EVERY MONDAY EVENING, RAIN OR SHINE. I'M CERTAIN SHE KNEW IT WAS ONE OF MY FAVORITES.

Preparation and cooking time: 1 to 1½ hours

Yield: 3—4 servings

⅓ cup / 75 mL all-purpose flour
4 cups / 1 L stock of your choice
¾ pound / 375 g fresh okra
2 cups / 500 mL cooked callaloo
2 green onions, chopped (about ½ cup / 125 mL)

2 cups / 500 mL milk
¼ cup / 60 mL butter
1 teaspoon / 5 mL salt
½ teaspoon / 2 mL black pepper

IN a small bowl, whisk together the flour and ½ cup / 125 mL of the stock until free of lumps. Set aside.

WASH the okra gently but thoroughly in cold water. In a small saucepan, cover the okra with water. Cook over medium heat for 15 to 20 minutes or until they are tender-crisp. Drain and rinse under cold water to cool. Remove and discard the okra tips and stems, then slice the okra into thin circles. Set aside.

IN a medium saucepan over low heat, cook the callaloo and green onions in 2 tablespoons / 25 mL water for 3 minutes or until the green onions are soft. In a food processor, purée the callaloo and onion mixture. Transfer to a stockpot.

ADD the remaining stock and heat over medium-high heat for 2 minutes. Reduce the heat to low and pour in the milk and the flour mixture. Simmer, stirring frequently, for another 15 minutes. Don't boil. Stir in the okra, butter, salt, and pepper, stirring until the butter is melted. Serve hot.

JAMAICAN BEEF AND VEGETABLE SOUP

ASK ANY JAMAICAN WHEN THE HURRICANE SEASON IS EXPECTED TO ROLL IN AND THEY TELL YOU, "JUNE COME TOO SOON, JULY STAND BY, AUGUST IT'S A MUST, SEPTEMBER A TIME TO REMEMBER, OCTOBER IT'S ALL OVER." THIS ISLAND DISH IS JUST AS PREDICTABLE, AS IT'S PREPARED IN MOST JAMAICAN HOMES. ENJOY THIS SOUP AS A MEAL IN ITSELF OR WITH A GREEN SALAD AND CRUSTY BREAD.

Preparation and cooking time: 1 to 2 hours

Yield: 6–8 servings

8 cups / 2 L water
1 pound / 500 g stewing beef or soup bones
1 large onion, chopped (about 1½ cups / 375 mL)
2 cloves garlic, chopped (about 1 tablespoon / 15 mL)
½ teaspoon / 2 mL salt
2 large carrots, chopped (about 2 cups / 500 mL)
2 potatoes, chopped (about 2 cups / 500 mL)
2 cups / 500 mL chopped cabbage
2 cups / 500 mL diced pumpkin
2 stalks celery, chopped (about 2 cups / 500 mL)

2 cups / 500 mL fresh or canned tomatoes, chopped
1 cup / 250 mL fresh or canned corn kernels
½ cup / 125 mL chopped mushrooms
1 (1-ounce/ 28-g) packet beef noodle soup mix
2 green onions, chopped (about ½ cup / 125 mL)
1 Scotch bonnet pepper
3 large sprigs of fresh thyme (or 1 teaspoon / 5 mL dried thyme)
2 tablespoons / 25 mL margarine or butter
½ teaspoon / 2 mL black pepper

IN a stockpot, bring the water to a rolling boil. Add the beef. Boil, skimming the scum as it forms on the surface, usually in the first 10 minutes of boiling. Add the onion, garlic, and salt. Cook until the beef is tender.

REDUCE the heat to medium and add the carrots, potatoes, cabbage, and pumpkin. Cover the pot and simmer for 10 minutes.

REDUCE the heat to low and add the celery, tomatoes, corn, and mushrooms. Simmer for 5 to 10 minutes or until the vegetables are cooked yet still crunchy.

ADD the beef soup mix, green onions, Scotch bonnet pepper, thyme, margarine, and black pepper. Simmer for another 10 minutes.

DISCARD the Scotch bonnet pepper (don't burst it) and thyme sprigs. Serve hot with your favorite bread.

FRESH CREAM CORN SOUP

THIS SOUP CAME ABOUT AFTER I ORDERED THE FRESH CORN SOUP AT A FINE LANDMARK RESTAURANT OUTSIDE BOSTON. IT BROUGHT BACK SO MANY CHILDHOOD MEMORIES THAT I DECIDED I HAD TO MAKE IT FOR MYSELF. OF COURSE, I GOT A LITTLE HELP FROM MY MOTHER.

Preparation and cooking time: 45 minutes to 1 hour

Yield: 3–4 servings

2 cups / 500 mL milk
¼ cup / 60 mL all-purpose flour
3 cups / 750 mL canned or frozen corn, puréed
¼ cup / 60 mL butter
1 onion, finely chopped (about 1 cup / 250 mL)

1 cup / 250 mL heavy cream
½ teaspoon / 2 mL salt
¼ teaspoon / 1 mL white pepper
1 sprig of parsley for garnish

IN a medium saucepan scald the milk. Set aside ½ cup / 125 mL of the milk. In a small bowl whisk together another ½ cup / 125 mL of the milk and the flour, whisking until free of lumps. Set aside.

ADD the corn to the milk in the saucepan and cook over low heat, stirring occasionally, for 5 minutes. Set aside.

IN a medium skillet over medium heat, melt the butter. Add the onions and sauté until they are soft. Add the onions to the corn mixture; stir well. Stir the flour mixture into the corn mixture. Add the reserved ½ cup / 125 mL milk, the cream, salt, and pepper. Simmer over low heat for 5 minutes or until heated through; don't allow it to boil.

GARNISH with parsley and serve immediately with your favorite bread.

VEGETABLE SOUP

THIS WAS ANOTHER ONE OF MY CREATIONS FOR OUR VEGETARIAN CUSTOMERS. THIS RECIPE TOOK A LOT OF TRIAL AND ERROR BEFORE MY FRIENDS AND FAMILY GAVE ME THE THUMBS-UP. I WOULD LOVE TO GET YOUR FEEDBACK ONCE YOU GIVE IT A TRY.

Preparation and cooking time: 1 hour

Yield: 3–4 servings

2 onions, chopped (about 2 cups / 500 mL)
4 cloves garlic, chopped (about 2 tablespoons / 25 mL)
2 tablespoons / 25 mL butter
3 cups / 750 mL water
3 to 4 vegetable bouillon cubes
2 stalks celery, chopped (about 2½ cups / 625 mL)
1 large carrot, sliced (about 1 cup / 250 mL)
2 green onions, chopped (about ¾ cup / 175 mL)

1 cup / 250 mL finely chopped fresh or canned tomatoes
1 cup / 250 mL cubed potato
2 teaspoons / 10 mL sugar
½ teaspoon / 2 mL thyme leaves
½ teaspoon / 2 mL salt
½ teaspoon / 2 mL black pepper
1 Scotch bonnet pepper
1 cup / 250 mL coarsely chopped cabbage

PUT the onions, garlic, and butter in a large skillet. Place the skillet on medium heat and sauté the onions and garlic until the onions are limp. Set aside.

IN a stockpot, bring the water to a rolling boil. Stir in the onion mixture, the bouillon cubes, celery, carrot, green onions, tomatoes, potatoes, sugar, thyme, salt, and black pepper. Cover the pot, reduce heat to low, and simmer for 5 minutes. Add the Scotch bonnet pepper and cabbage, cover the pot, and simmer for another 5 to 10 minutes or until the cabbage is tender.

DISCARD the Scotch bonnet pepper (don't burst it). Serve with your favorite bread.

SALADS

~~~~~~~~~

"BETTA BELLY BUS DAN GOOD BICKLE WAYSE"

Better to eat till discomfort than
to waste good food.

JAMAICAN POTATO SALAD

HERE'S A DECORATIVE AND SATISFYING SALAD FOR ANY OCCASION.

Preparation and cooking time: 1 hour   Yield: 6–8 servings

4 cups / 1 L diced cooked potatoes
  (about 2 pounds / 1 kg)
1½ cups / 375 mL green peas
1 cup / 250 mL peeled and diced cucumber
  (about 1 cucumber)
I cup / 250 mL thinly sliced celery (about 1 stalk)
½ cup /125 mL grated carrots (about 1 carrot)
3 green onions, chopped (about ¾ cup / 175 mL)

1½ cups / 375 mL mayonnaise
1 tablespoon / 15 mL white vinegar
1 teaspoon / 5 mL salt
½ teaspoon / 2 mL white pepper
I head lettuce
1 green pepper cut in rings (remove white membranes)
  for garnish
1 tomato cut in wedges for garnish

IN a large bowl combine the potatoes, peas, cucumber, celery, carrots, green onions, mayonnaise, vinegar, salt, and white pepper; toss together well. (If not using salad immediately, cover and refrigerate.)

JUST before serving, wash and dry the lettuce. Shred the lettuce and arrange on a serving platter. Spoon the salad on top and garnish with the green pepper rings and tomato wedges.

KOOL SALAD

THIS RECIPE IS SURE TO GIVE YOU AND YOUR FRIENDS A NEW APPRECIATION FOR CABBAGE AND CUCUMBERS. IT'S GUARANTEED TO RIVAL THE BEST COLESLAW YOU'VE EVER TASTED.

Preparation time: 30 to 40 minutes　　　　　　　　　**Yield: 10–12 servings**

4 cups / 1 L shredded cabbage
2 cups / 500 mL shredded carrots
3 large cucumbers, diced

2 green peppers, diced (about 3 cups / 750 mL)
5 green onions, finely chopped (about 1 cup / 250 mL)

Dressing
¾ cup / 175 mL white vinegar
½ cup / 125 mL mayonnaise
¼ cup / 60 mL sugar
¼ cup / 60 mL canola oil

1 teaspoon / 5 mL salt
½ teaspoon / 2 mL finely chopped Scotch bonnet pepper
¼ teaspoon / 1 mL black pepper
2 cloves garlic, crushed (about 1 tablespoon/ 15 mL)

IN a large salad bowl toss together the cabbage, carrots, cucumbers, green peppers, and green onions.

PUT all the dressing ingredients in a sealable container, cover tightly, and shake well until the sugar dissolves. Pour the dressing over the vegetables and toss the salad once more. Chill for 6 to 8 hours before serving.

CARROT AND CABBAGE SALAD

THIS SALAD IS A FAVORITE IN ALMOST ALL JAMAICAN HOMES. IT IS LOADED WITH ANTIOXIDANTS AND FIBER, BUT DON'T LET THAT STOP YOU FROM ENJOYING ITS WONDERFUL FLAVOR.

Preparation time: 30 minutes

Yield: 6 servings

12 whole lettuce leaves, washed and dried
3 cups / 750 mL shredded cabbage

2 cups / 500 mL shredded carrots

Vinaigrette
½ cup / 125 mL olive oil
½ cup / 125 mL white vinegar
2 teaspoons / 10 mL sugar

1 teaspoon / 5 mL salt
¼ teaspoon / 1 mL black pepper

CUT the white stems off the lettuce leaves. Line each of 6 salad plates or salad bowls with 2 of the leaves. Spread ½ cup / 125 mL of the shredded cabbage over each plate. Then spread one-third cup / 75 mL of the shredded carrot in a layer on each plate.

PUT all the vinaigrette ingredients in a sealable container, cover tightly, and shake until the sugar and salt dissolve. Sprinkle the vinaigrette on the salads. Chill for 15 minutes and serve.

AVOCADO SALAD

THIS COOL YET TANGY SALAD IS GUARANTEED TO BE A HIT AS AN APPETIZER OR A SIDE DISH AT YOUR NEXT BARBECUE.

Preparation and cooking time: 20 minutes

Yield: 2–3 servings

1 large avocado, cubed (about 2 cups / 500 mL)
2 green onions, chopped (about ½ cup / 125 mL)
2 tablespoons / 25 mL mayonnaise
1 teaspoon / 5 mL lime juice

½ teaspoon / 2 mL finely chopped fresh parsley
½ teaspoon / 2 mL garlic salt
½ teaspoon / 2 mL hot pepper sauce

IN a salad bowl, combine the avocado, green onions, mayonnaise, lime juice, parsley, garlic salt, and hot pepper sauce; toss well. Chill before serving.

FRESH GREEN BEAN SALAD

PRETTY MUCH ALL OF THE RURAL HOUSES IN JAMAICA HAVE A VEGETABLE GARDEN WITH BEANS LINING THE FENCES. TO AVOID SPOILAGE, MANY RECIPES HAVE BEEN CREATED OVER THE YEARS. THIS SALAD IS ONE OF THEM.

Preparation time: 30 to 40 minutes (not including marinating time)   Yield: 6–8 servings

2 pounds / 1 kg fresh green beans, trimmed

Vinaigrette

½ cup / 125 mL red wine vinegar
½ cup / 125 mL olive oil
2 teaspoons / 10 mL sugar
1 teaspoon / 5 mL finely chopped fresh parsley
1 teaspoon / 5 mL salt

½ teaspoon / 2 mL black pepper
¼ teaspoon / 1 mL hot pepper sauce
1 small onion, thinly sliced
2 cloves garlic, finely chopped (about 1 tablespoon / 15 mL)

CUT each bean in two. In a large saucepan, cover the beans with water and bring to a rolling boil. Turn off the heat and leave the beans to sit in the hot water for 5 minutes. The beans should still be crunchy.

MEANWHILE, in a large bowl whisk together all the vinaigrette ingredients until the sugar and salt dissolve.

DRAIN the beans and toss them in the vinaigrette while they are still hot. Cover and set aside at room temperature to marinate for about 2 hours.

SPICY CUCUMBER SALAD

I USED TO THINK THIS SALAD — MY FAVORITE AS A CHILD — WAS MADE IN EVERY HOME. BUT RECENTLY WHEN I MENTIONED CUCUMBER SALAD TO A JAMAICAN FRIEND, SHE HAD NEVER HEARD OF IT. WHEN I ASKED MY MOTHER ABOUT THE ORIGIN OF THIS SALAD, SHE TOLD ME IT WAS A FAMILY RECIPE.

THIS SALAD IS GREAT WITH FRIED OR BARBECUED MEATS OR FISH.

Preparation time: 30 minutes

Yield: 6–8 servings

3 large cucumbers, thinly sliced
1 large onion, thinly sliced
½ teaspoon / 2 mL finely chopped hot pepper

½ teaspoon / 2 mL salt
¼ teaspoon / 1 mL black pepper

IN a large sealable container, combine the cucumbers, onion, hot pepper, salt, and black pepper. Cover tightly and shake well for 2 minutes. Chill for about 15 minutes before serving.

SPICY SALTED CODFISH SALAD

THIS RECIPE IS A MUST-TRY IF YOU LIKE SPICY SALADS. IT WAS A POPULAR ITEM ON THE MENU AT OUR RESTAURANTS; TASTE FOR YOURSELF WHY.

Preparation time: 30 minutes

Yield: 6–8 servings

1 large head iceberg or romaine lettuce
2 large tomatoes, diced
1 large green pepper, chopped
1 large cucumber, thinly sliced
6 large red radishes, thinly sliced

1 large onion, thinly sliced
2 cloves garlic, finely chopped (about 1 tablespoon / 15 mL)
½ pound / 250 g salted codfish, desalted, deboned, and shredded*

Vinaigrette
¾ cup / 175 mL white vinegar
¼ cup / 60 mL sugar
¼ cup / 60 mL vegetable oil
1 teaspoon / 5 mL salt

1 teaspoon / 5 mL hot pepper sauce
½ teaspoon / 2 mL finely chopped hot pepper
¼ teaspoon / 1 mL black pepper

* *For desalting codfish, see page 38.*

WASH and dry the lettuce leaves. Tear the lettuce into bite-sized pieces and place them in a large sealable container. Chill the salad until you are ready to serve it.

JUST before serving, make the vinaigrette. In a sealable container combine the vinegar, sugar, vegetable oil, salt, hot pepper sauce, hot pepper, and black pepper. Cover tightly and shake well until the sugar and salt dissolve.

TO the lettuce add the tomatoes, green pepper, cucumbers, radishes, onion, garlic, and codfish. Pour on the vinaigrette and toss the salad. Serve immediately.

MAIN COURSES

~~~~~~~~~~~~~~~~~~~~

"DI NEARA DI BONE
DI SWEETA DI MEAT"

The nearer to the bone,
the sweeter the meat.

WORKING with FISH

Desalting Dried Salted Fish

PUT the fish in a medium saucepan and add enough cold water to cover. Boil the fish for 15 minutes. Drain the fish and rinse with cold water. If it's still salty, cover it again with cold water and boil it for another 10 minutes.

YOU can also soak the fish in cold water overnight. Pour off the soaking water, add fresh cold water, and boil for 5 minutes.

Buying Fresh Fish

WHEN selecting fresh fish, make certain its flesh is firm and elastic and its eyes and gills are red or pink. It should smell fresh. Fresh fish sinks when placed in water.

Preparing Fresh Fish

WHEN cleaning fish, always wash it with water and lemon or lime juice, or water and vinegar. When cleaning up counters and cooking surfaces, use a slice of lemon or lime with your cleaning agent to eliminate any fish odor.

Sewing Fish

YOU will need a large needle and thread to sew up your fish after you have stuffed its cavity. You want to make tight stitches, but be careful not to pull too firmly on the thread or you will tear the skin. If you do tear the skin on your first try, "dinner is not ruined." Simply make new stitches farther into the body of the fish. If you do not have a needle, you can wrap your fish tightly with kitchen string or thread. Remove the stitches or thread before serving.

ACKEE AND SALTED CODFISH

THIS IS JAMAICA'S NATIONAL DISH. ACKEE IS THE SUBJECT OF MANY SONGS AND MUCH FOLKLORE. WE OFTEN SAY THAT ACKEE IN ITS POD LOOKS LIKE A FACE THAT STARES AT YOU AS YOU GO BY THE STANDS IN THE MARKET. ACKEE'S SCIENTIFIC NAME, *BLIGHIA SAPIDA*, COMES FROM FAMED BRITISH SEA CAPTAIN WILLIAM BLIGH (*MUTINY ON THE BOUNTY*). BLIGH BROUGHT THE PLANT TO JAMAICA FROM WEST AFRICA IN 1793.

Preparation and cooking time: 30 to 45 minutes   **Yield: 4–5 servings**

2 cups / 500 mL fresh ackee or 1 (19-ounce / 540-mL) can*
¼ cup / 60 mL canola or vegetable oil
1 large onion, sliced
1 tomato, chopped (about ½ cup / 125 mL)

¼ teaspoon / 1 mL minced Scotch bonnet pepper
½ pound / 250 g salted codfish, desalted, deboned, and cooked**
½ teaspoon / 2 mL black pepper
Salt to taste (if using fresh ackee)

*If you are using canned ackee, you do not need to boil it. Simply drain the ackee and add it to the skillet after sautéing the fish.
**For desalting codfish, see page 38.

IN a large saucepan, bring to a rolling boil enough water to cover the fresh ackee. Carefully add the fresh ackee and cover the pot. Boil until the ackee is soft but not mushy, about 15 minutes. Drain the ackee and set it aside.

IN a medium skillet over medium heat, heat the oil. Sauté the onion, tomato, and Scotch bonnet pepper until the onions are limp. Fold in the codfish, reduce the heat to low, and simmer for 5 to 10 minutes or until the water from the codfish evaporates.

PUSH the codfish mixture to one side of the skillet. Place the cooked or canned ackee on the other side, then scoop the codfish mixture over the ackee. Simmer for 4 to 6 minutes or until the water from the ackee evaporates. Sprinkle with ¼ teaspoon / 1 mL of the black pepper. Using a spatula, carefully fold the ackee over once, being careful not to mash it. Sprinkle with the remaining black pepper.

WHEN serving, use a slotted spoon to leave behind the excess oil. Serve with rice, boiled or fried green bananas (page 88), fried dumplings (page 85), or fried or roasted breadfruit.

STUFFED BREADFRUIT WITH ACKEE AND SALTED CODFISH

CAPTAIN WILLIAM BLIGH, OF *BOUNTY* FAME, INTRODUCED BREADFRUIT TO JAMAICA IN 1793. HISTORIANS REPORT THAT 347 BREADFRUIT TREES WERE BROUGHT ON THE HMS *PROVIDENCE* AS FOOD FOR SLAVES. TODAY, BREADFRUIT PROVIDES AMPLE STARCH IN THE JAMAICAN DIET. IT IS COMMONLY SERVED AS A SIDE DISH WITH ACKEE AND SALTFISH.

Preparation and cooking time: 2 to 2½ hours

Yield: 5–6 servings

1 breadfruit
Ackee and Salted Codfish (page 39)

2 tablespoons / 25 mL margarine

REMOVE the breadfruit stem and wash the breadfruit. Insert a sharp knife in the center of the stem almost to the bottom of the fruit. This will help to speed up the cooking. Put enough water in a stockpot to submerge the breadfruit. Remove the breadfruit and bring the water to a rolling boil. Carefully place the breadfruit in the boiling water and cook for 30 minutes. Drain the breadfruit and allow it to cool.

PREHEAT the oven to 325°F / 160°C.

PEEL the skin from the breadfruit. Cut a thin slice from the bottom of the breadfruit so it stands upright. Place the breadfruit on its side on a cutting board and slice off the top 1 inch / 2.5 cm. Set the top aside. Use a tablespoon to core out the heart (middle) of the breadfruit. Discard the heart.

FILL the breadfruit with the ackee and salted codfish filling. Replace the top and smear the entire fruit with half of the margarine. Place the breadfruit upright in a large roasting pan and cover with foil.

BAKE the breadfruit until a knife can be inserted easily, 30 to 40 minutes. Smear the remaining margarine over the breadfruit. Return the breadfruit to the oven and broil until golden brown. Serve hot.

CALLALOO AND SALTED CODFISH

THIS IS A REGULAR SUNDAY-MORNING JAMAICAN BREAKFAST, USUALLY SERVED WITH HARD DOUGH BREAD OR BOILED GREEN BANANAS (PAGE 88). YOU CAN USE AN EQUAL AMOUNT OF SPINACH AS A SUBSTITUTE FOR CALLALOO.

Preparation and cooking time: 20 to 30 minutes　　　　　　　　**Yield: 2 servings**

1 large bundle callaloo or 1 (19-ounce / 540-mL) can
2 tablespoons / 25 mL vegetable oil
1 large onion, sliced
1 tomato, diced (about ½ cup / 125 mL)
½ teaspoon / 2 mL finely chopped Scotch bonnet pepper

¼ pound / 125 g salted codfish, desalted and deboned*
1 teaspoon / 5 mL garlic powder
½ teaspoon / 2 mL black pepper
½ teaspoon / 2 mL salt

For desalting codfish, see page 38.

CLEAN and dry the callaloo. Chop the leaves and stalks into small pieces and set aside.

IN a medium skillet over medium heat, heat the oil. Sauté the onion, tomato, and Scotch bonnet pepper until the vegetables are tender. Fold in the salted codfish, garlic powder, and black pepper. Cover the skillet and reduce the heat to low. Simmer for about 5 minutes. Fold in the callaloo and salt. Cover and simmer until the callaloo is tender. Remove the cover and simmer for 5 minutes or until some of the juices evaporate. The finished dish should be wet but not watery.

SERVE with breadfruit, rice, or boiled green bananas (page 88).

CALLALOO AND SALTED CODFISH— STUFFED BAKED POTATOES

YOU WILL LOVE THE TASTE AND APPRECIATE THE SIMPLICITY OF THIS ONE-DISH MEAL. YOU CAN USE AN EQUAL AMOUNT OF SPINACH AS A SUBSTITUTE FOR CALLALOO.

Preparation and cooking time: 1 hour   Yield: 2–4 servings

2 tablespoons / 25 mL butter
1 small onion, diced (about ½ cup / 125 mL)
1 small tomato, diced (about ½ cup / 125 mL)
½ cup / 125 mL fresh or canned callaloo
¼ teaspoon / 1 mL minced hot pepper
¼ pound / 125 g salted codfish, desalted, deboned, and cooked*

¼ teaspoon /1 mL black pepper
2 tablespoons / 25 mL milk
2 large baked potatoes
½ teaspoon / 2 mL paprika

*For desalting codfish, see page 38.

PREHEAT the oven to 325°F / 160°C.

IN a medium saucepan over medium heat, melt 1 tablespoon / 15 mL of the butter. Sauté the onion, tomato, callaloo, and hot pepper until the callaloo and onions are soft. Reduce heat to low and add the codfish and black pepper; simmer for 5 minutes. Remove from the heat and stir in the milk and remaining 1 tablespoon / 15 mL butter.

CUT the potatoes in half lengthwise. Spoon the flesh into a bowl, leaving a thin layer next to the skin. Put the potato skins on a baking sheet and set aside. Mash the potato flesh until smooth, then stir in the fish mixture. Spoon the potato mixture into the potato skins and sprinkle with paprika.

BAKE for 8 to 10 minutes or until heated through. Serve hot.

SALTED CODFISH AND CALLALOO OMELET

SALTED CODFISH WAS ONCE USED AS CURRENCY FOR PURCHASING SLAVES. TODAY, SALTFISH IS MORE COMMON THAN BUTTER IN MOST JAMAICANS' DIETS. HERE, THE FISH AND CALLALOO MAKE IT A NUTRITIOUS MEAL. YOU CAN USE AN EQUAL AMOUNT OF SPINACH AS A SUBSTITUTE FOR CALLALOO.

Preparation and cooking time: 20 to 30 minutes   **Yield: 1–2 servings**

1 tablespoon / 15 mL butter
1 small onion, diced (about ½ cup / 125 mL)
1 green onion, chopped (about ¼ cup / 60 mL)
¼ cup / 60 mL cooked callaloo
¼ teaspoon / 1 mL minced Scotch bonnet pepper (optional)
¼ pound / 125 g salted codfish, desalted, deboned, cooked, and shredded*

¼ teaspoon / 1 mL black pepper
¼ teaspoon / 1 mL dried thyme
3 eggs
2 tablespoons / 25 mL milk
2 teaspoons / 10 mL vegetable oil

For desalting codfish, see page 38.

In a medium skillet over medium heat, melt the butter. Sauté the onion, green onion, callaloo, and Scotch bonnet pepper until the callaloo and onions are soft. Add the codfish, black pepper, and thyme. Cook, stirring, for 2 to 3 minutes, then set aside.

Beat the eggs lightly and add the milk. In a medium skillet over medium heat, heat the oil. When it is hot, pour in the egg mixture. When the eggs are set and light brown on the bottom, scoop the fish mixture onto one half of the omelet; fold the other half over to cover the fish. Let the omelet cook for 2 minutes. Flip and cook for another 2 minutes. Serve hot.

SALTED CODFISH HASH

WHEN I first came to Canada and tried hash browns I must confess I didn't care much for the taste. I decided that the challenge would be to make something similar using potatoes, but with a little more flavor. Being a lover of salted codfish, I thought this would be a great marriage. Can you taste any reason why these two should not be together?

Preparation and cooking time: 20 to 30 minutes ·   Yield: 3–4 servings

½ pound / 250 g salted codfish, desalted, deboned, cooked, and shredded*
2 small potatoes, boiled and finely chopped (about ½ cup / 125 mL)

1 small onion, grated (about ½ cup / 125 mL)
1 tablespoon / 15 mL butter, melted
½ teaspoon / 2 mL black pepper
2 teaspoons / 10 mL vegetable oil

*For desalting codfish, see page 38.

In a bowl combine the codfish, potatoes, onion, butter, and black pepper. Place a medium skillet over medium heat and allow it to get hot. Add the oil. When the oil is hot, drop heaping tablespoons of the hash mixture into the skillet, flattening each cake lightly with a spatula. Reduce the heat to medium-low and cook the hash until the bottoms are light brown. Turn over and cook the other side until light brown. Serve hot.

BAKED SALTED CODFISH AND BLACK-EYED PEAS

WITHOUT A DOUBT, THE MOST POPULAR JAMAICAN BEAN DISH IS JAMAICAN RICE AND PEAS. HOWEVER, SEVERAL TYPES OF PEAS (BEANS) ARE COMMON TO THE ISLAND. IN FACT, AS FAR BACK AS 500 B.C., JAMAICA'S FIRST NATIVES, THE ARAWAK INDIANS, ARE BELIEVED TO HAVE EATEN BEANS, INCLUDING LIMA BEANS AND BLACK-EYED PEAS, WHICH GREW WILD ON THE ISLAND.

Preparation and cooking time: 30 to 40 minutes   Yield: 4–5 servings

2 tablespoons / 25 mL butter or vegetable oil
1 large onion, chopped (about 1½ cups / 375 mL)
2 cloves garlic, chopped (about 1 tablespoon / 15 mL)
1 large tomato, chopped (about 2 cups / 500 mL)
½ teaspoon / 2 mL salt
¼ teaspoon / 1 mL black pepper
2 tablespoons / 25 mL tomato paste
1 tablespoon / 15 mL molasses

½ teaspoon / 2 mL finely chopped Scotch bonnet pepper (optional)
2 cups / 500 mL cooked black-eyed peas, rinsed and drained if canned
1½ cups / 375 mL shredded, cooked, desalted, and deboned salted codfish*
½ cup / 125 mL dry bread crumbs or finely crushed peanuts for topping

*For desalting codfish, see page 38.

PREHEAT the oven to 350°F / 180°C.

IN a medium saucepan over medium heat, melt the butter. Sauté the onion, garlic, tomato, salt, and black pepper until the onions are limp. Mix in the tomato paste, molasses, and Scotch bonnet pepper. Stir in the black-eyed peas. Turn the mixture out into a medium casserole dish and bake for 15 minutes.

SPREAD the codfish on top. Do not stir. Sprinkle on the topping of your choice, then bake for another 15 to 20 minutes or until the top is brown. Serve hot.

SALTED CODFISH AND SWEET POTATO CASSEROLE

SWEET POTATOES GROW EVERYWHERE ON THE ISLAND AND ARE A PART OF EVERY JAMAICAN'S DIET. THE ORANGEY-RED SKINS ARE USUALLY THIN, AND THE FLESH IS DENSER THAN THAT OF NORTH AMERICAN SWEET POTATOES, WHICH MEANS THEY USUALLY TAKE LONGER TO COOK. THEIR DENSE TEXTURE PERFECTLY SUITS THIS RECIPE, AS THE LONGER COOKING TIME ALLOWS THE SEASONINGS TO BLEND WITH THE POTATOES' SWEETNESS.

Preparation and cooking time: 30 minutes

Yield: 5–6 servings

6 sweet potatoes (sweet yams), peeled
½ teaspoon / 2 mL salt
1 (10-ounce/ 284-mL) can condensed cream of celery soup
2 onions, sliced

½ pound / 250 g salted codfish, desalted, deboned, and shredded*
2 tablespoons / 25 mL butter, melted
1 cup / 250 mL crushed cornflakes
½ cup / 125 mL grated Parmesan cheese

*For desalting codfish, see page 38.

COOK the potatoes in a large pot of boiling salted water until tender. Drain the potatoes and let cool. Slice them into ½-inch / 1-cm thick rounds.

PREHEAT the oven to 375°F / 190°C.

SPREAD a layer of potato slices in the casserole dish. Top with a thin layer of condensed soup, then some of the onions and salted codfish. Repeat this layering, ending with a layer of potato slices. Brush the top with butter.

COVER and bake for 15 minutes. Sprinkle with the cornflakes, then sprinkle on the grated cheese. Bake, uncovered, another 15 minutes or until the cheese is melted. Cut into serving portions. Serve hot.

SALTED MACKEREL WITH GREEN BANANAS

I CAN THINK OF TWO REASONS WHY SALTED MACKEREL WITH GREEN BANANAS IS A STAPLE MEAL FOR MOST JAMAICANS. THE FIRST IS OBVIOUS: IT HAS A WONDERFULLY SPICY TASTE. THE SECOND IS MORE PRACTICAL: THE INGREDIENTS DO NOT HAVE TO BE REFRIGERATED AND CAN BE KEPT FOR WEEKS BEFORE BEING PREPARED. THIS WAS VERY IMPORTANT IN THE PAST, SINCE MANY JAMAICANS LIVED WITHOUT REFRIGERATORS.

Preparation and cooking time: 1 hour   **Yield: 5–6 servings**

¼ cup / 60 mL canola or vegetable oil
1 large onion, sliced
1 large tomato, chopped (about 2 cups / 500 mL)

1 teaspoon / 5 mL minced hot pepper
3 pounds / 1.5 kg salted mackerel, desalted and cooked*
½ teaspoon / 2 mL black pepper

*For desalting mackerel, see page 38.

HEAT the oil in a medium skillet over medium heat. Sauté the onions, tomato, and hot pepper until the onions are limp. Scoop the vegetables and oil into a bowl and set aside.

REDUCE heat to low and place the mackerel in the skillet. Cover with the sautéed vegetables and oil. Cover the skillet and simmer until all the water from the mackerel evaporates. Remove from the heat and sprinkle with black pepper.

USING a slotted spoon to eliminate the excess oil, transfer the mackerel to plates. Serve with boiled green bananas (page 88).

BROWN STEW FISH

ALMOST ALL JAMAICANS PREPARE THIS RECIPE, NOT SO MUCH FOR THE NUTRITIONAL VALUE BUT BECAUSE OF THE WAY THE FISH ABSORBS THE SEASONINGS AND SPICES. SERVE THIS DELICIOUS FISH WITH BOILED BANANAS OR DUMPLINGS OR ON A BED OF RICE.

Preparation and cooking time: 1 hour

Yield: 3–4 servings

2 eggs, beaten
1 cup / 250 mL seasoned dry bread crumbs (or plain bread crumbs mixed with ½ teaspoon / 2 mL each salt and black pepper)
1 lime
1 (3–5-pound / 1.5–2.5-kg) whole snapper or kingfish (or equivalent weight in steaks)
1 teaspoon / 5 mL salt
½ teaspoon / 2 mL black pepper
½ teaspoon / 2 mL paprika

2 cups / 250 mL vegetable oil
2 tablespoons / 25 mL butter
1 onion, chopped (about 1 cup / 250 mL)
1 tomato, diced (about 1½ cups / 375 mL)
2 green onions, chopped (about ½ cup /125 mL)
1 small green pepper, chopped (about 1 cup / 250 mL)
2 sprigs of fresh thyme (or ½ teaspoon / 2 mL dried thyme)
1 Scotch bonnet pepper
1 cup / 250 mL rich brown sauce (page 137)
½ teaspoon / 2 mL ground allspice

PLACE the beaten eggs and bread crumbs in 2 separate shallow bowls large enough to dip the fish in. Squeeze the lime juice over the fish; let it sit for a couple of minutes and then rinse with cold water. Dry the fish with paper towels and rub inside and out with the salt, pepper, and paprika. Dip the fish in the eggs and drain off any excess egg. Then coat the fish with the bread crumbs and shake off any excess crumbs. Set the breaded fish aside for 30 minutes.

PLACE a medium skillet over medium heat. When it is hot, add about ½ inch / 1 cm oil. When the oil is hot, carefully add the breaded fish. Fry the fish for no more than 5 or 6 minutes per side, until it is golden brown and the flesh is white and flaky. Drain the fish on paper towels.

MELT the butter in a medium saucepan over medium heat. Sauté the onion, tomato, green onions, green pepper, thyme, and Scotch bonnet pepper until the onions are limp (don't burst the pepper). Stir in the rich brown sauce and allspice. Remove from the heat.

PLACE the fish in a large skillet and pour the brown sauce mixture over it. Simmer the fish over medium-low heat for 15 minutes, turning it once during that time. Remove sprigs of thyme before serving. Serve the fish and sauce with white rice, potatoes, or boiled green bananas (page 88).

ESCOVITCH FISH

THE CULTURAL INFLUENCE OF THE FIRST SPANISH SETTLERS IN THE FIFTEENTH CENTURY IS A VITAL PART OF JAMAICA'S HISTORY. OF THE MANY FOODS THEY INTRODUCED, THE MOST CHERISHED IS ESCOVITCH FISH. THE WORD "ESCOVITCH" COMES FROM THE SPANISH WORD *ESCABECHE*, WHICH MEANS "PICKLED." IN JAMAICA, THIS DISH IS PREPARED AS A MEAL AT HOME OR BOUGHT AS A SNACK FROM STREET VENDORS.

Preparation and cooking time: 1 hour

Yield: 6–7 servings

1 lime
4 pounds / 2 kg whole fish or fish steaks
2 teaspoons / 10 mL salt
1 teaspoon / 5 mL black pepper
Vegetable oil for frying

3 large onions, thinly sliced
1 Scotch bonnet pepper, chopped
1½ cups / 375 mL white vinegar
2 tablespoons / 25 mL vegetable oil
½ teaspoon / 2 mL salt

SQUEEZE the lime juice over the fish; let it sit for a couple of minutes and then rinse with cold water. Dry the fish with paper towels. Season it inside and out with the salt and pepper.

PLACE a medium skillet on medium heat. When it is hot, add ½ inch / 1 cm oil. When the oil is hot but not smoking, carefully add the fish. Fry the fish on both sides for 5 minutes or until it is golden brown and the flesh is white and flaky. Drain the fish on paper towels.

IN a small saucepan combine the onions, Scotch bonnet pepper, vinegar, 2 tablespoons / 25 mL oil, and salt. Bring to a rolling boil, then remove from the heat. Put the fish in a serving dish and pour the vinegar dressing on top. Cover the dish to moisten the fish through condensation and seal in the flavor. Serve hot or cold.

BAKED WHOLE FISH

THE MOST POPULAR FISH CAUGHT IN THE WATERS OF JAMAICA INCLUDE MARLIN, WHICH PRODUCES GOOD STEAKS; KINGFISH, A LARGER MEATY FISH; PARROT FISH; GROUPER; MULLET, A FRESHWATER FISH; AND SNAPPER, WHICH IS THE MOST COMMON. ALL OF THE STUFFING RECIPES IN THIS BOOK COMPLEMENT FISH NICELY, ALTHOUGH MY OWN FAVORITE IS CALLALOO STUFFING (PAGE 91).

Preparation and cooking time: 1 hour

Yield: 6–7 servings

1 lime
1 (3–5-pound / 1.5–2.5-kg) whole fish (such as snapper, kingfish, or jackfish)
½ teaspoon / 2 mL salt
½ teaspoon / 2 mL black pepper
Stuffing of your choice (pages 89–91)
¼ cup / 60 mL melted butter or vegetable oil to brush on fish

PREHEAT the oven to 450°F / 230°C. Lightly grease a baking dish large enough to hold the fish.

SQUEEZE the lime juice over the fish; let it sit for a couple of minutes and then rinse with cold water. Pat the fish dry and rub it with salt and pepper inside and out. Stuff the fish with the stuffing and carefully sew the cavity closed (see page 38). Place the fish in the baking dish and brush it with the melted butter.

BAKE for 10 minutes to seal in the juices. Reduce the heat to 425°F / 220°C and bake for 30 to 40 minutes or until the flesh is white and flaky, occasionally basting the fish with oil or melted butter. A good timing gauge is 10 minutes per pound / 500 g up to 4 pounds / 2 kg and 5 minutes for each additional pound.

BAKED WHOLE FISH WITH CALLALOO STUFFING

I HAVE MANY FOND MEMORIES OF EATING THIS DISH IN JAMAICA. WE USED TO DRIVE OUT TO A RESTAURANT ON THE PALIZADOES (NOW NORMAN MANLEY) AIRPORT ROAD TO ENJOY THEIR STUFFED FISH ON A PATIO THAT WAS ALMOST IN THE OCEAN. IT WAS AFTER WE MOVED TO CANADA THAT I DECIDED TO RECREATE THIS RECIPE.

Preparation and cooking time: 1 to 1½ hours

Yield: 6–8 servings

1 lime
1 (3–5-pound / 1.5–2.5-kg) whole fish (such as snapper)
½ teaspoon / 2 mL salt
½ teaspoon /2 mL black pepper
Callaloo Stuffing (page 91)
¼ cup / 60 mL melted butter or vegetable oil

PREHEAT the oven to 450°F / 230°C. Grease a baking sheet.

SQUEEZE the lime juice over the fish; let it sit for a couple of minutes and then rinse with cold water. Dry the fish with paper towels and season it inside and out with the salt and pepper. Stuff the fish with Callaloo Stuffing and carefully sew the cavity closed (see page 38). Place the fish on the baking sheet and brush it with the melted butter.

BAKE for 10 minutes to seal in the juices. Reduce the heat to 400°F / 200°C and bake for 30 to 45 minutes or until the flesh is white and flaky, occasionally basting the fish with oil or melted butter. A good timing gauge is 10 minutes per pound / 500 g up to 4 pounds / 2 kg and 5 minutes for each additional pound.

BAKED FISH WITH MUSHROOMS AND TOMATO

THIS WAS ONE OF MY CREATIONS FOR OUR VEGETARIAN CUSTOMERS. IT WAS ALSO ONE OF OUR MOST POPULAR DISHES WITH VEGETARIANS AND MEAT-LOVERS ALIKE.

Preparation and cooking time: 1 to 1½ hours   Yield: 5–6 servings

3 tablespoons / 45 mL butter
1 small onion, chopped (about ¼ cup / 60 mL)
1 cup / 250 mL sliced mushrooms
¼ cup / 60 mL chopped celery
1 cup / 250 mL dry bread crumbs
1 teaspoon / 5 mL salt

½ teaspoon / 2 mL black pepper
¼ teaspoon / 1 mL minced Scotch bonnet pepper
2 pounds / 1 kg fish fillets
1 tablespoon / 15 mL lemon juice
4 slices tomato
1 cup / 250 mL stock of your choice

PREHEAT the oven to 375°F / 190°C.

IN a medium saucepan over medium heat, melt the butter. Sauté the onions, mushrooms, and celery until the onions are limp. Add the bread crumbs, salt, black pepper, and Scotch bonnet pepper; mix together and set aside.

ARRANGE the fish in a large baking dish and sprinkle with the lemon juice. Cover the fish with the vegetable mixture, then with the tomato slices. Pour on the stock.

BAKE for 35 minutes or until the fish is white and flaky. Serve with your choice of potatoes.

CURRY BEEF

SOME PEOPLE SAY CURRIES DEFINE CARIBBEAN COOKING. CURRIES WERE INTRODUCED TO JAMAICA BY THE CHINESE AND EAST INDIAN IMMIGRANTS WHO CAME TO WORK IN THE PLANTATIONS AFTER THE SLAVE TRADE WAS ABOLISHED IN 1838. OVER THE YEARS JAMAICANS HAVE CURRIED EVERYTHING FROM MANGOES TO GOAT. THERE ARE MANY VARIATIONS IN THE SPICES USED IN CURRIES, RESULTING IN FLAVORS THAT RANGE FROM EXTREMELY HOT TO SWEET.

Preparation and cooking time: 1 hour (not including marinating)   Yield: 4–5 servings

3 pounds / 1.5 kg stewing beef, cut into 1-inch / 2.5-cm cubes
1 large onion, sliced
6 cloves garlic, finely chopped (about 3 tablespoons / 45 mL)
¼ Scotch bonnet pepper, finely chopped (about ½ teaspoon / 2 mL)
2 teaspoons / 10 mL Worcestershire sauce
1 teaspoon / 5 mL salt

1 teaspoon / 5 mL black pepper
3 large sprigs of fresh thyme (or 2 teaspoons / 10 mL dried thyme)
2 tablespoons / 25 mL vegetable or canola oil
1 teaspoon / 5 mL sugar
5 green onions, chopped (about 1 cup / 250 mL)
2 teaspoons / 10 mL curry powder
3 potatoes, peeled and cut into 1-inch / 2.5-cm cubes

WASH the beef in cold water and pat it dry. Place the beef in a sealable container and add the onion, garlic, Scotch bonnet pepper, Worcestershire sauce, salt, black pepper, and thyme. Wearing rubber gloves, rub the spices into the beef with your hands. Marinate, covered and refrigerated, for 1 to 2 hours.

IN a large pot over medium heat, heat the oil and sugar, stirring until the sugar is brown. Add the beef and marinade, green onions, and curry; stir thoroughly. Cover the pot, reduce the heat to low, and simmer the beef slowly in its own juices, stirring occasionally, for 30 minutes or until the beef is tender. If the meat is tough, pour ¼ cup / 60 mL of water at a time down the sides of the skillet, not directly onto the beef (or you will toughen the meat).

WHEN the beef is tender, add the potatoes and ¼ cup / 60 mL water; stir thoroughly. Cover and simmer for 10 minutes or until the potatoes are tender. Crush some of the potatoes to thicken the sauce, if desired. If there is not enough sauce, add ¼ cup / 60 mL water and simmer for another 5 to 10 minutes.

SERVE with rice or roti (page 84) and a salad.

CURRY CHICKEN

THERE ARE THREE COMMON METHODS FOR EATING CURRY DISHES. THE FIRST, AND MOST COMMON AMONG THE CARIBBEAN CULTURES, IS TO SERVE THE CURRY ON A BED OF RICE WITH VEGETABLES OR A SALAD. OTHER CARIBBEAN CULTURES SERVE CURRY IN A BOWL AND SCOOP IT OUT WITH PIECES OF ROTI; AND STILL OTHERS PREFER TO WRAP THE CURRY IN A ROTI TO CREATE A POUCH THAT IS EASY TO MANAGE AND EAT.

Preparation and cooking time: 1 hour (not including marinating)   Yield: 4–5 servings

1 (3–4-pound / 1.5–2-kg) chicken, cut into 8 serving pieces
1 onion, chopped (about 1 cup / 250 mL)
2 cloves garlic, crushed (about 1 tablespoon / 15 mL)
1 tablespoon / 15 mL curry powder

1 teaspoon / 5 mL dried thyme
1 teaspoon / 5 mL salt
½ teaspoon / 2 mL black pepper
3 potatoes, peeled and cut into ½-inch / 1-cm cubes
2 tablespoons / 25 mL butter or vegetable oil

WASH the chicken and place the chicken pieces in a large sealable container. Add the onion, garlic, curry powder, thyme, salt, and black pepper. Wearing rubber gloves, rub the spices into the chicken pieces with your hands. Marinate, covered and refrigerated, for 2 to 3 hours.

IN a large pot, combine the chicken and marinade, potatoes, and butter; stir well. Cover the pot and simmer over low heat, stirring occasionally, allowing the chicken to cook slowly in its own juices, for 30 minutes or until the chicken is cooked through and the potatoes are cooked but not too soft. If there is not enough sauce, add ¼ cup / 60 mL water and simmer for another 5 to 10 minutes.

MASH some of the potatoes to thicken the sauce, if desired.

SERVE curry hot with steamed rice, rice and peas (page 92), roti (page 84), or boiled green bananas (page 88).

CURRY GOAT

IN THE PAST, THIS DISH WAS PREPARED ONLY FOR GRAND CELEBRATIONS AND WEDDINGS, BUT AS PEOPLE BECAME MORE HEALTH-CONSCIOUS THEY BEGAN SERVING IT MORE FREQUENTLY. GOAT MEAT IS ONE OF THE HEALTHIER MEATS BECAUSE IT IS SO LOW IN FAT.

Preparation and cooking time: 1 to 1½ hours (not including marinating)   Yield: 4–5 servings

3 pounds / 1.5 kg goat, cut into 1-inch / 2.5-cm cubes
1 lime
1 large onion, sliced
6 cloves garlic, finely chopped
    (about 3 tablespoons / 45 mL)
2 teaspoons / 10 mL salt
1 teaspoon / 5 mL black pepper

1 teaspoon / 5 mL thyme leaves
¼ teaspoon / 1 mL finely chopped Scotch bonnet pepper
2 tablespoon / 25 mL canola or vegetable oil
1 teaspoon / 5 mL sugar
5 green onions, chopped (about 1 cup / 250 mL)
2 teaspoons / 10 mL curry powder
2 potatoes, peeled and cut into ½-inch / 1-cm cubes

SQUEEZE the lime juice over the goat; let it sit for a couple of minutes and then rinse with cold water. Drain off excess water. Place the goat in a sealable container and add the onion, garlic, salt, black pepper, thyme, and Scotch bonnet pepper. Wearing rubber gloves, rub the spices into the goat with your hands. Marinate, covered and refrigerated, for 1 to 2 hours.

IN a large pot over medium heat, heat the oil and sugar, stirring until the sugar is brown. Add the goat with marinade, green onions, and curry; stir thoroughly. Cover the pot, reduce the heat to low, and simmer the goat slowly in its own juices, stirring occasionally, until the goat is nearly tender, about 30 minutes. If the meat is tough, pour ¼ cup / 60 mL of water at a time down the sides of the pot, not directly onto the goat (or you will toughen the meat).

ADD the potatoes and ¼ cup / 60 mL water; stir thoroughly. Cover and simmer for 15 minutes or until the potatoes are cooked but not too soft. Crush some of the potatoes to thicken the sauce, if desired. If there is not enough sauce, add ¼ cup / 60 mL water and simmer for another 5 to 10 minutes.

SERVE with rice or roti (page 84) and a salad.

CURRY SHRIMP

THIS CURRY SHRIMP RECIPE IS DIFFERENT FROM ALL OTHER CURRY SHRIMP RECIPES. THE FLAVORFUL BLEND OF SPICES, SEASONINGS, AND CURRY IS DELECTABLE ON ITS OWN. BUT IT'S THE POTATOES THAT PULL THE SEASONINGS, CURRY, AND SHRIMP TOGETHER, WHILE MAKING IT THAT MUCH MORE OF A HEARTY DISH.

Preparation and cooking time: 30 to 45 minutes   Yield: 3–4 servings

2 potatoes, cut into ½-inch / 1-cm cubes
1 large onion, chopped (about 1½ cups / 375 mL)
4 cloves garlic, chopped (about 2 tablespoons / 25 mL)
½ cup / 125 mL water
¼ cup /60 mL vegetable oil
1 teaspoon / 5 mL curry powder

1 teaspoon / 5 mL salt
1 teaspoon / 5 mL hot pepper sauce
½ teaspoon / 2 mL thyme leaves
½ teaspoon / 2 mL sugar
½ teaspoon / 2 mL black pepper
1 pound / 500 g shrimp, peeled

IN a large pot, combine the potatoes, onion, garlic, water, oil, curry powder, salt, hot pepper sauce, thyme, sugar, and black pepper. Over medium heat, bring to a simmer and cook for about 20 minutes, stirring occasionally, until the potatoes are tender. Fold in the shrimp, cover the pot, and simmer for another 2 to 3 minutes or until the shrimp are just cooked. Mash some of the potatoes to thicken the sauce, if desired.

SERVE curry hot on white rice or roti (page 84).

CURRY POTATO

I DEVELOPED THIS RECIPE FOR MY VEGETARIAN CUSTOMERS, WHO WANTED A CURRY THEY TOO COULD ENJOY. I USED POTATOES BECAUSE THEY ARE THE COMMON DENOMINATOR IN MOST CURRY DISHES. WHAT MAKES ME MOST PROUD IS THAT EVERYONE, INCLUDING MEAT-LOVERS, ENJOYS THIS DISH.

Preparation and cooking time: 30 to 45 minutes

Yield: 2–3 servings

2 potatoes, peeled and cut into ½-inch / 1-cm cubes
1 large onion, chopped (about 1½ cups / 375 mL)
4 cloves garlic, chopped (about 2 tablespoons / 25 mL)
3 green onions, chopped (about ¾ cup / 175 mL)
2 large sprigs of fresh thyme (or ½ teaspoon / 2 mL dried thyme)
¼ cup / 60 mL vegetable oil

1 teaspoon / 5 mL sugar
1 teaspoon / 5 mL finely chopped Scotch bonnet pepper
½ teaspoon / 2 mL curry powder
½ teaspoon / 2 mL salt
½ teaspoon / 2 mL black pepper
½ cup / 125 mL water
1 tablespoon / 15 mL butter

IN a large pot combine the potatoes, onion, garlic, green onions, thyme, oil, sugar, Scotch bonnet pepper, curry powder, salt, and black pepper. Add the water and stir well. Bring to a rolling boil, reduce the heat to low, cover the pot, and simmer, stirring occasionally, for 20 to 30 minutes or until the potatoes are tender. Don't overcook. Fold in the butter until melted and remove from the heat. Mash some of the potatoes to thicken the sauce, if desired.

REMOVE sprigs of thyme before serving. Serve curry hot on its own or with rice or roti (page 84) and a salad.

CURRY BARBECUED CHICKEN

JAMAICANS BARBECUE YEAR ROUND. UNLIKE NORTH AMERICANS, SOME JAMAICANS USE WOOD (INSTEAD OF CHARCOAL) AND THEY ALWAYS MARINATE THEIR MEATS IN VARIOUS WELL-SEASONED AND SPICED MARINADES. IF YOUR TASTE BUDS ARE GAME, I SUGGEST YOU TRY THIS RECIPE WITH THE SCOTCH BONNET PEPPER. BY THE WAY, KEEP A BOWL OF SUGAR HANDY: IT IS THE BEST WAY TO COOL A BURNING TONGUE.

Preparation and cooking time: 1 hour (not including marinating)   **Yield: 4–5 servings**

1 (3–5-pound / 1.5–2.5-kg) chicken, cut into 8 pieces
1½ cups / 375 mL plain yogurt
½ cup / 125 mL lime juice
2 teaspoons / 10 mL ground coriander
2 teaspoons / 10 mL grated ginger
1 teaspoon / 5 mL lime zest

1 teaspoon / 5 mL paprika
1 teaspoon / 5 mL curry powder
1 teaspoon / 5 mL salt
½ teaspoon / 2 mL finely chopped Scotch bonnet pepper (optional)
4 cloves garlic, finely chopped (about 2 tablespoons / 25 mL)

WASH and drain the chicken and place it in a sealable container. In a bowl, stir together the yogurt, lime juice, coriander, ginger, lime zest, paprika, curry powder, salt, Scotch bonnet pepper, and garlic. Pour over the chicken, turning to coat the chicken. Marinate, covered and refrigerated, for at least 8 hours (overnight is great), turning the chicken once while marinating.

PREHEAT the broiler or grill.

REMOVE the chicken from its marinade. Broil or barbecue the chicken for 10 to 15 minutes or until chicken is no longer pink at the bone, basting frequently with the marinade. (Do not leave the marinade at warm temperatures for more than 5 minutes.)

FLOURED CURRY CHICKEN

GOAT IS THE MOST POPULAR MEAT IN JAMAICA, BUT TODAY MANY HOUSEHOLDS ARE PREPARING CHICKEN BECAUSE IT IS LESS EXPENSIVE TO RAISE AND EASIER TO PREPARE — COMPARED TO SLAUGHTERING A GOAT!

Preparation and cooking time: 1½ hours

Yield: 4–5 servings

1 (3–5-pound / 1.5–2.5-kg) chicken, cut into 8 pieces
All-purpose flour to coat
½ cup / 125 mL butter
1 small onion, chopped (about ¼ cup / 60 mL)
1 small green pepper, chopped (about 1 cup / 250 mL)
4 cloves garlic, finely chopped
   (about 2 tablespoons / 25 mL)

1 teaspoon / 5 mL curry powder
½ teaspoon / 2 mL dried thyme
1 tomato, chopped (about 1½ cups / 375 mL)
1 teaspoon / 5 mL sugar
1 teaspoon / 5 mL black pepper
Salt to taste

WASH the chicken and pat dry. Lightly coat each chicken piece with the flour, shaking off any excess flour.

IN a large, deep skillet over medium heat, melt the butter. Fry the chicken for about 5 minutes or until it is golden brown on all sides. Transfer the chicken to a large casserole dish.

PREHEAT the oven to 350°F / 180°C.

USING the same skillet, heat the chicken drippings over medium heat. Sauté the onion, green pepper, garlic, curry powder, and thyme until the onions are limp. Add the tomato, sugar, pepper, and salt. Reduce heat to low and simmer for 5 minutes. Pour the mixture over the chicken.

BAKE for 1 hour or until the chicken is cooked through. Serve with rice.

CURRY POTATO STUFFING

I CREATED THIS RECIPE BECAUSE I WANTED A TASTY STUFFING FOR POULTRY, BUT YOU CAN ALSO SERVE IT AS A SIDE DISH OR WITH ROTI, RICE, OR GREEN BANANAS.

Preparation and cooking time: 30 to 45 minutes

Yield: 3–4 servings

¼ cup / 60 mL dry bread crumbs
1 cup / 250 mL stock of your choice
2 tablespoons / 25 mL vegetable oil or butter
1 onion, chopped (about 1 cup / 250 mL)
1 green onion, chopped (about ¼ cup / 60 mL)
2 cloves garlic, chopped (about 1 tablespoon / 15 mL)

2 potatoes, diced (about 2 cups / 500 mL)
1 teaspoon / 5 mL curry powder
½ teaspoon / 2 mL salt
½ teaspoon / 2 mL black pepper
1 large sprig of fresh thyme (or ½ teaspoon / 2 mL dried thyme)

STIR together the bread crumbs and ½ cup / 125 mL of the stock. Set aside.

IN a medium skillet over medium heat, melt the butter. Sauté the onion, green onion, and garlic until the onions are limp. Mix in the potatoes, the remaining ½ cup / 125 mL stock, curry powder, salt, black pepper, and thyme. Reduce the heat to low, cover the skillet, and simmer until the potatoes are almost cooked, 10 to 15 minutes. Fold in the soaked bread crumbs; simmer for another 5 to 8 minutes or until the potatoes are cooked through but not mushy. Remove the sprig of thyme before using stuffing.

CURRY FISH

ASK YOUR FISHMONGER FOR SNAPPER, GROUPER, OR KINGFISH. ALL ARE WELL SUITED TO THIS RECIPE AND ARE WHAT YOU'D FIND IN JAMAICA.

Preparation and cooking time: 1 hour (including marinating)   Yield: 3–4 servings

1 lime
2 pounds / 1 kg fish steaks or fillets
½ teaspoon / 2 mL salt
½ teaspoon / 2 mL black pepper
2 tablespoons / 25 mL vegetable oil or butter
1 onion, chopped (about 1 cup / 250 mL)

2 cloves garlic, chopped (about 1 tablespoon / 15 mL)
1 small tomato, chopped (about ½ cup / 125 mL)
1 small green pepper, chopped (about 1 cup / 250 mL)
¼ teaspoon / 1 mL dried thyme
1 teaspoon / 5 mL curry powder
3–4 tablespoons / 45–60 mL water

SQUEEZE the lime juice over the fish; let it sit for a couple of minutes and then rinse with cold water. Pat the fish dry. Rub the salt and black pepper over the fish inside and out. Marinate the fish, covered and refrigerated, for 30 minutes.

IN a medium skillet over medium heat, heat the oil. Sauté the onion, garlic, tomato, green pepper, and thyme until the onions are limp. Stir in the curry powder. Push the vegetable mixture to one side of the skillet. Place the fish in the skillet and scoop the mixture over the fish. Pour the water down the side of the skillet, not directly onto the fish. Cover the skillet and simmer for 10 to 15 minutes or until the fish is white and flaky.

SERVE curry hot with white rice, boiled green bananas (page 88), or ugali (page 93).

SALTED CODFISH-EGG CURRY

IN JAMAICA, THIS DISH IS USUALLY SERVED ON BEN JOHNSON'S DAY — THE DAY BEFORE PAY DAY — WHEN GROCERIES ARE LOW AND THERE ISN'T ENOUGH TO FEED THE FAMILY.

Preparation and cooking time: 20 to 30 minutes

Yield: 3–4 servings

½ pound / 250 g salted codfish, deboned, desalted, and cooked*
3 hard-boiled eggs
2 tablespoons / 25 mL vegetable oil or butter
1 small onion, chopped (about ¼ cup / 60 mL)

1 green onion, chopped (about ¼ cup / 60 mL)
1 small tomato, diced (about ½ cup / 125 mL)
¼ teaspoon / 1 mL finely chopped hot pepper
½ teaspoon / 2 mL curry powder
¼ teaspoon / 1 mL black pepper

*For desalting codfish, see page 38.

SHRED the salted codfish and set it aside. Dice the eggs and set them aside.

IN a medium saucepan over medium heat, heat the oil. Sauté the onion, green onion, tomato, and hot pepper until the onions are limp. Stir in the curry powder and black pepper. Fold in the codfish and eggs. Cover the pan, reduce the heat to low, and simmer for 5 minutes.

SERVE hot with bread or dumplings (pages 85–86).

AFRICAN BEEF PEANUT STEW

AFRICAN SLAVES IMPORTED TO BRITISH-COLONIZED JAMAICA BETWEEN 1655 AND 1838 BROUGHT WITH THEM SUCH DISHES AS CHAPATI AND UGALI. (JAMAICANS CALL THESE DISHES ROTI AND TURN CORNMEAL, RESPECTIVELY.) ALTHOUGH THIS AFRICAN BEEF PEANUT STEW IS NOT CONSIDERED AUTHENTIC JAMAICAN CUISINE TODAY, IT'S A WONDERFUL DISH FROM A LINEAGE THAT IS AT THE HEART OF THE ISLAND'S CULTURE.

Preparation and cooking time: 45 minutes to 1 hour (not including marinating)   Yield: 4–5 servings

2 pounds / 1 kg stewing beef, cut into
   1-inch / 2.5-cm cubes
2 onions, chopped (about 2 cups / 500 mL)
4 cloves garlic, finely chopped
   (about 2 tablespoons / 25 mL)

1 teaspoon / 5 mL salt
1 teaspoon / 5 mL black pepper
2 tablespoons / 25 mL butter or vegetable oil
2 cups / 500 mL milk
1 cup / 250 mL peanut butter of your choice

WASH the beef and drain off any excess water. In a sealable container combine the beef with the onions, garlic, salt, and black pepper; mix well. Marinate, covered and refrigerated, for 1 hour.

HEAT the oil in a medium saucepan over medium heat. Remove the beef from its marinade and set the marinade aside, refrigerated. Place the beef in the saucepan, cover the pan, and reduce the heat to medium-low. Cook for about 30 minutes or until the beef is tender, stirring occasionally. If the juices evaporate, pour no more than ¼ cup / 60 mL water at a time down the side of the pan, not directly onto the meat (or you will toughen the meat).

ADD the marinade, milk, and peanut butter, and stir until the peanut butter dissolves. Simmer, stirring occasionally, until the sauce thickens. If the stew is too thick, gradually stir in a little milk or water until you have the consistency you desire. The stew should not be watery.

SERVE with steamed rice or ugali (page 93).

FRESH CORN AND BEEF STEW

GARLIC IS USED IN ALMOST ALL OF JAMAICA'S SAVORY DISHES. MANY JAMAICANS SAY WE HAVE THE SPANISH TO THANK FOR GARLIC'S PROMINENT POSITION IN THE ISLAND'S COOKING.

Preparation and cooking time: 1½ hours (not including marinating)　　　　**Yield: 3–4 servings**

1 pound / 500 g stewing beef,
　　cut in ½-inch / 1-cm cubes
1 onion, finely chopped (about 1 cup / 250 mL)
4 cloves garlic, crushed (about 2 tablespoons / 25 mL)
1½ teaspoons / 7 mL Worcestershire sauce
1 teaspoon / 5 mL salt

1 teaspoon / 5 mL black pepper
3 tablespoons / 45 mL butter or margarine
2 cups / 500 mL kernel corn (fresh, canned, or frozen)
1 cup / 250 mL rich brown sauce (page 137)
3 tablespoons / 45 mL dry bread crumbs

RINSE the beef in cold water and drain off any excess water. In a sealable container, mix the beef with the onion, garlic, Worcestershire sauce, salt, and pepper; mix well. Marinate, covered and refrigerated, for about 2 hours.

PREHEAT the oven to 350°F / 180°C. Grease a medium casserole dish.

IN a medium skillet over medium heat, melt the butter. Sauté the corn for 2 minutes. In the casserole dish, alternate layers of corn and beef with its marinade, beginning and ending with the corn. Pour the rich brown sauce over top. Cover the casserole dish and bake for 1½ hours or until the meat is tender.

SPRINKLE with the bread crumbs and bake, uncovered, for 20 minutes or until the bread crumbs are golden brown. Serve hot.

OXTAIL AND LIMA BEAN STEW

STEWS ARE VERY COMMON IN JAMAICAN CUISINE. THIS IS A LEGACY FROM THE AFRICAN SLAVES BROUGHT TO THE ISLAND DURING THE SLAVE TRADE THAT BEGAN IN THE 1600s. THEY PUT TO USE THEIR SKILL OF FORAGING FOR LOCAL INGREDIENTS AND BOILING THEM UP INTO HEARTY ONE-POT MEALS.

Preparation and cooking time: 2 to 3 hours

Yield: 4–5 servings

3½ pounds / 1.75 kg oxtail, cut at the joint
  by your butcher
2 large onions, chopped (about 3 cups / 750 mL)
6 cloves garlic, chopped (about 3 tablespoons / 45 mL)
2 tablespoons / 25 mL soy sauce
1 teaspoon / 5 mL salt

1 large tomato, diced (about 2 cups / 500 mL)
1 (16-ounce / 454-g) can lima beans, drained and rinsed
2 sprigs of fresh thyme (or 1 teaspoon / 5 mL dried thyme)
2 tablespoons / 25 mL butter
1 teaspoon / 5 mL black pepper

WASH the oxtail in cold water. In a stockpot, combine the oxtail, half of the onions, the garlic, soy sauce, and salt. Add enough water to come halfway up the oxtail. Bring to a rolling boil, occasionally skimming the scum as it forms, usually in the first 10 minutes of boiling. Reduce the heat and simmer until the oxtail is tender, about 1½ hours.

ONCE the oxtail is tender, there should be about 2 cups / 500 mL of liquid in the stockpot. If the liquid level is low, add enough to make 2 cups / 500 mL. Add the remaining onion, tomato, lima beans, thyme, butter, and black pepper. Cover and simmer for 10 to 15 minutes or until the lima beans are hot but not mushy. Remove the thyme sprigs before serving.

SERVE hot with white rice and boiled green bananas (page 88).

BROWN STEW PORK

TWO WORDS BEST DESCRIBE THIS DISH: "COMFORT FOOD." COMPARED TO JERK PORK, THIS RECIPE IS MUCH EASIER TO PREPARE BUT EQUALLY DELICIOUS. EVEN NOW, WHEN I GO TO MY MOTHER'S HOME IN JAMAICA, OR WHEN SHE VISITS, SHE ALWAYS PREPARES THIS DISH FOR ME. THIS IS MOM'S RECIPE. YOU CAN USE ANY CUT OF PORK.

Preparation and cooking time: 1 to 1½ hours (not including marinating)   Yield: 4–5 servings

2 pounds / 1 kg pork, cut into 2-inch / 5-cm cubes
2 onions, chopped (about 2 cups/ 500 mL)
4 green onions, chopped (about 1 cup / 250 mL)
4 cloves garlic, chopped (about 2 tablespoons / 25 mL)
1 tablespoon / 15 mL finely chopped fresh ginger
1 teaspoon / 5 mL salt
1 teaspoon / 5 mL black pepper

½ teaspoon / 2 mL dried thyme
2 tablespoons / 25 mL vegetable oil
1 tomato, diced (about 1½ cups / 375 mL)
1 Scotch bonnet pepper (optional)
2 teaspoons / 10 mL soy sauce
½ cup / 125 mL water

TRIM the excess fat from the pork and wash the meat thoroughly; drain off any excess water. Put the pork in a sealable container and add the onions, green onions, garlic, ginger, salt, black pepper, and thyme. Wearing rubber gloves, massage the seasonings into the meat with your hands. Marinate, covered and refrigerated, for 2 to 3 hours.

HEAT the oil in a large saucepan over medium heat. Remove the pork from the marinade (reserving the marinade) and in batches brown the pork thoroughly on all sides. Once the pork is brown, remove it from the saucepan and pour off all the fat.

RETURN the pork to the saucepan. Add the marinade, tomato, hot pepper, soy sauce, and ¼ cup / 60 mL of the water. Cover and simmer slowly on low heat, stirring occasionally, for 30 to 40 minutes or until the pork is tender. If the liquid evaporates, add no more than ¼ cup / 60 mL water at a time down the side of the pan, not directly onto the pork (or you will toughen the meat).

WHEN the pork is cooked, add the remaining ¼ cup / 60 mL water and simmer for another 5 to 8 minutes. Allow the water to reduce slightly and absorb the seasonings to produce a thicker and more flavorful sauce. Discard the Scotch bonnet pepper (don't burst it) before serving.

JERK PORK

JERK IS A JAMAICAN METHOD OF SLOWLY COOKING SPECIALLY SEASONED MEATS OVER A SMOKING FIRE. IT EVOLVED FROM THE DAYS WHEN BUCCANEERS HUNTED THE ISLAND'S WILD PIGS (IN THE EIGHTEENTH CENTURY). THE KEY INGREDIENTS ARE PIMENTO (WHOLE ALLSPICE) AND SCOTCH BONNET PEPPERS. ROADSIDE VENDORS COOK JERK MEATS IN CUSTOM-MADE STEEL DRUMS THAT ARE CUT IN HALF LENGTHWISE TO MAKE A SMOKING PIT.

Preparation and cooking time: 1 hour (not including marinating)   Yield: 5–6 servings

⅓ cup / 75 mL vegetable oil
¼ cup / 60 mL vinegar
3 tablespoons / 45 mL thyme leaves
2 tablespoons / 25 mL pimento seeds (allspice)
2 tablespoons / 25 mL finely chopped fresh ginger
2 tablespoons / 25 mL lime juice
1 tablespoon / 15 mL ground allspice
2 teaspoons / 10 mL salt

2 teaspoons / 10 mL black pepper
1 teaspoon / 5 mL brown sugar
½ teaspoon / 2 mL cinnamon
6 green onions
6 large cloves garlic
½ Scotch bonnet pepper
3 pounds / 1.5 kg pork leg, cut in 2-inch / 5-cm cubes

IN a bowl combine the oil, vinegar, thyme, pimento seeds, ginger, lime juice, ground allspice, salt, black pepper, sugar, and cinnamon. Chop the green onions, garlic, and Scotch bonnet pepper as finely as possible and add to the oil mixture; stir well.

WASH the pork thoroughly in cold water and drain off any excess water. Add the pork to the spice mixture and, wearing rubber gloves, rub the spice mixture thoroughly into the pork with your hands. Marinate, covered and refrigerated, at least 5 hours or overnight.

PREHEAT the oven to 350°F / 180°C. Grease a baking sheet.

SPREAD the marinated pork on the baking sheet. Bake the pork for 30 to 45 minutes or until it is brown and cooked throughout, turning the pork frequently for even browning. Discard the pimento seeds before serving.

SERVE as a meal with rice and peas (page 92) or as finger food with Jamaican hard dough bread or regular sourdough bread. Or make jerk pâté (page 12).

PORK MARINADE

THIS VERSATILE MARINADE SUITS ANY CUT OF PORK AND CAN BE USED FOR GRILLING OR PANFRYING. MIGHT I SUGGEST YOU TRY THE JAMAICAN "PICK-A-PEPPER" HOT SAUCE WHEN YOU ARE PREPARING THIS RECIPE? IT IS NOT AS HOT AS THE SCOTCH BONNET PEPPER, BUT IT STILL OFFERS A NICE FLAVOR AND A WOW-OF-KICK.

Preparation time: 10 minutes (not including marinating)　　　　Yield: ¾ cup / 175 mL

¼ cup / 60 mL chili sauce of your choice
3 tablespoons / 45 mL lime juice
1 tablespoon / 15 mL grated onion
2 teaspoons / 10 mL Worcestershire sauce

½ teaspoon / 2 mL salt
½ teaspoon / 2 mL paprika
½ teaspoon / 2 mL dried chili flakes (optional)
¼ teaspoon / 1 mL black pepper

COMBINE the chili sauce, lime juice, onion, Worcestershire sauce, salt, paprika, chili flakes, and black pepper.

MARINATE any cut of pork for 3 to 4 hours. Cook it however you wish, basting the pork frequently with the marinade.

REMEMBER that any marinade that has been used for meat, poultry, or fish should not be left at room temperature for more than 5 minutes.

PORK, SHRIMP, AND RICE COOK-UP

WHEN I was growing up, "cook-up" usually meant a one-dish meal or cooking with few pots, which made clean-up easy. As a teen I had many cookouts with my brothers and friends by the river that ran through our farm. We had easy access to all kinds of meats from the farm and we'd catch shrimp straight from the river. In place of the pork, try tender beef or chicken.

Preparation and cooking time: 30 to 45 minutes (not including marinating)   Yield: 5–6 servings

1 pound / 500 g boneless pork, cut in 1-inch / 2.5-cm cubes
1 teaspoon / 5 mL paprika
½ teaspoon / 2 mL black pepper
1 teaspoon / 5 mL salt
2 cups / 500 mL long-grain rice
3 cups / 750 mL water

3 tablespoons / 45 mL coconut cream
3 tablespoons / 45 mL vegetable oil or margarine
2 onions, chopped (about 2 cups / 500 mL)
1 tomato, chopped (about 1½ cups / 375 mL)
½ pound / 250 g shrimp, peeled and deveined
2 green onions, chopped (about ½ cup / 125 mL)
1 teaspoon / 5 mL Worcestershire sauce

In a sealable container combine the pork, paprika, pepper, and ½ teaspoon / 2 mL of the salt. Wearing rubber gloves, massage the seasonings into the pork with your hands. Marinate, covered and refrigerated, for at least 30 minutes.

In a large pot, combine the rice, water, coconut cream, and remaining ½ teaspoon / 2 mL salt. Bring to a rolling boil, stirring to blend in the coconut cream. Reduce the heat to low, cover the pot, and simmer until the rice is cooked, about 20 minutes. Set the rice aside.

Meanwhile, in a large saucepan over medium heat, heat the oil. Stir-fry the marinated pork until the pork is lightly browned on the outside. Add the onions and tomato, and stir-fry until the pork is no longer pink inside.

Add the shrimp and cook for 2 to 3 minutes or until the shrimp turn pink. Reduce the heat to medium-low. Add the cooked rice, green onions, and Worcestershire sauce; toss gently. Cover and simmer for 5 minutes or until the rice is heated through.

Serve hot with buttered squash or stir-fried vegetables.

JERK CHICKEN

THIS RECIPE WAS GIVEN TO ME IN 1980 DURING MY VACATION IN OCHO RIOS, WHILE I WAS AT A JERK CHICKEN COOKOUT ON THE BEACH AT ONE OF THE FINER HOTELS. THE JERK CHICKEN WAS BEING SOLD FOR $20 U.S. I OFFERED THE CHEF $20, NOT FOR CHICKEN BUT FOR THE RECIPE, AND HE ACCEPTED. BACK HOME, I IMPROVED THE RECIPE AND HAVE USED IT EVER SINCE.

Preparation and cooking time: 1 hour (not including marinating)   Yield: 5–6 servings

1 (3–4-pound / 1.5–2-kg) chicken, cut into 8 pieces
⅓ cup / 75 mL vegetable oil
¼ cup / 60 mL white vinegar
2 tablespoons / 25 mL lime juice
1 tablespoon / 15 mL ground allspice
1 tablespoon / 15 mL pimento seeds (allspice)
2 teaspoons / 10 mL salt
2 teaspoons / 10 mL black pepper

1 tablespoon / 15 mL finely chopped ginger
1 teaspoon / 5 mL brown sugar
½ teaspoon / 2 mL ground cinnamon
3 large sprigs of fresh thyme (or 1 teaspoon / 5 mL dried thyme)
5 green onions
2 large cloves garlic
½ Scotch bonnet pepper

WASH the chicken pieces and drain the excess water. In a bowl combine the oil, vinegar, lime juice, ground allspice, pimento seeds, salt, black pepper, ginger, sugar, cinnamon, and thyme. Chop (do not blend) the green onions, garlic, and Scotch bonnet pepper as finely as possible; add to the oil mixture and stir well.

ADD the chicken to the spice mixture and, wearing rubber gloves, massage the spice mixture into the chicken with your hands. Marinate, covered and refrigerated, for at least 5 hours or overnight.

PREHEAT the oven to 350°F / 180°C. Grease a baking sheet.

SPREAD the marinated chicken on the baking sheet. Cover with foil and bake for 30 minutes or until the chicken is just cooked through. Remove the foil and broil the chicken until browned, turning once for even browning. Don't overcook. Discard the pimento seeds and thyme sprigs before serving.

SERVE hot or cold with Jamaican hard dough bread or regular sourdough bread.

THIS dish can also be cooked on a barbecue. Grill for 10 to 15 minutes or until the chicken is no longer pink at the bone, basting with the remaining marinade.

AFRICAN PILI PILI CHICKEN

EARLIER IN LIFE I ATTENDED MANY AFRICAN DIGNITARY FUNCTIONS AND NOTICED THIS DISH WAS SERVED AT MANY OF THEM. OF COURSE I HAD TO GET THE RECIPE AND WAS FORTUNATE ENOUGH TO FIND A CHEF AT ONE OF THE FUNCTIONS WHO WAS WILLING TO SHARE IT.

Preparation and cooking time: 1 to 1½ hours (not including marinating)   **Yield: 4–6 servings**

2 onions, grated (about 1⅓ cups / 325 mL)
6 cloves garlic, crushed (about 3 tablespoons / 45 mL)
½ Scotch bonnet pepper, finely minced
  (about 2 teaspoons / 10 mL)
1 cup / 250 mL ketchup
½ can beer (about 6 ounces/ 175 mL)
½ cup / 125 mL vegetable oil

¼ cup / 60 mL white vinegar
3 tablespoons / 45 mL garam masala
2 tablespoons / 25 mL water
1 teaspoon / 5 mL salt
½ teaspoon / 2 mL black pepper
12 pieces chicken

IN a sealable container combine the onions, garlic, Scotch bonnet pepper, ketchup, beer, oil, vinegar, garam masala, water, salt, and black pepper; mix well. Wash the chicken pieces and drain the excess water. Add the chicken pieces to the marinade, turning to coat well. Marinate, covered and refrigerated, for 3 to 4 hours.

PREHEAT the oven to 350°F / 180°C.

TURN the chicken and marinade into a roasting pan. Cover and roast for 30 to 45 minutes or until the chicken is no longer pink at the bone.

REMOVE the chicken from the roasting pan and set the juices aside. Grill the chicken on a barbecue (or broil) for 10 to 15 minutes or until brown, basting it frequently with the juices.

SERVE hot with rice and a salad of your choice.

VEGETABLES
~~~~~~~~~~~~~~

"OLE WOMAN A SWEAR FI
CALLALOO AN CALLALOO A
SWEAR FI RUN IM BELLY"

Be anxious for nothing.

BAKED CHOCHO (IRISH POTATO)

ON ITS OWN, CHOCHO IS RATHER BLAND, BUT IT SOAKS UP FLAVOR FROM THE HERBS AND SPICES IT'S COOKED WITH. WITH THIS IN MIND, THINK OF CHOCHO AS A CLEAN CANVAS WAITING FOR YOU TO CREATE A DELECTABLE MASTERPIECE.

Preparation and cooking time: 20 to 30 minutes

Yield: 6 servings

3 large chochos or potatoes (about 1½ pounds / 750 g)
1 tablespoon / 15 mL margarine
1 small onion, finely chopped (about ½ cup / 125 mL)
¼ cup / 60 mL ground beef

¼ teaspoon / 1 mL salt
¼ teaspoon / 1 mL black pepper
½ cup / 125 mL shredded cheddar cheese
⅓ cup / 75 mL dry bread crumbs

Cook the chochos in a pot of boiling salted water until they are cooked through but still firm. Drain the chochos, then cut them in half lengthwise. Scrape the flesh into a bowl, leaving a thin layer for a shell. Arrange the shells on a baking sheet and set aside. Mash the flesh and set it aside.

In a medium skillet over medium heat, melt the margarine. Sauté the onions until they are limp. Stir in the ground beef, salt, and pepper; simmer, stirring frequently, until the beef is no longer pink. Remove from the heat and stir in the mashed chochos. Reduce the heat to medium-low, cover the pan, and simmer for 5 minutes.

Meanwhile, preheat the broiler.

Fill the chocho shells with the beef mixture. In a bowl, combine the cheese and bread crumbs. Sprinkle over the filled chocho shells. Broil the chochos until the cheese is melted, about 2 to 3 minutes.

STEAMED CABBAGE

SERVE THIS COMFORTING DISH AS A DINNER SIDE DISH OR AS A BREAKFAST MEAL WITH BOILED GREEN BANANAS OR FRIED DUMPLINGS. DEBONED SALTED CODFISH, BOILED OR FRIED CRISPY, CAN ALSO BE ADDED TO THIS DISH.

Preparation and cooking time: 30 minutes

Yield: 2–3 servings

1 small cabbage (about 1 pound / 500 g), chopped
2 tablespoons / 25 mL butter or vegetable oil
1 onion, chopped (about 1 cup / 250 mL)
1 small tomato, chopped (about ½ cup / 125 mL)

½ pound / 250 g mushrooms, quartered
1 carrot, julienned (about ½ cup / 125 mL)
½ teaspoon / 2 mL salt
¼ teaspoon / 1 mL black pepper

WASH the cabbage in cold salted water, then rinse thoroughly in fresh cold water. Set cabbage aside. Melt the butter in a medium saucepan over medium heat. Sauté the onion and tomato until the onions are limp. Stir in the cabbage, mushrooms, carrot, salt, and pepper. Reduce the heat to low, cover, and simmer for 5 to 10 minutes or until the vegetables are cooked yet still crispy.

COCONUT VEGETABLES (JAMAICAN RUNDUN)

A TRADITIONAL DISH COMMONLY THOUGHT OF AS A POOR MAN'S MEAL IN JAMAICA, RUNDUN WAS ALWAYS A POPULAR MEAL ON MY RESTAURANTS' MENUS. RUNDUN TRANSLATES AS "RUN DOWN," ANOTHER WAY OF SAYING SIMMER DOWN. HERE, COCONUT MILK IS SIMMERED DOWN TO A CREAMY SAUCE FOR THE SAUTÉED VEGETABLES. SAUTÉED SHRIMPS CAN ALSO BE ADDED TO THIS RECIPE.

Preparation and cooking time: 30 to 45 minutes   **Yield: 4–5 servings**

2 tablespoons / 25 mL butter
3 green onions, chopped (about ¾ cup / 175 mL)
1 large onion, chopped (about 1½ cups / 375 mL)
1 tomato, diced (about 1½ cups / 375 mL)
½ pound / 250 g mushrooms, quartered
1 (14-ounce / 398-mL) can coconut milk
3 carrots, thinly sliced diagonally
   (about 1½ cups / 375 mL)

1 stalk celery, sliced diagonally
1 cup / 250 mL broccoli florets
½ pound / 250 g green beans
2 sprigs of fresh thyme (or 1 teaspoon / 5 mL dried thyme)
½ teaspoon / 2 mL finely chopped Scotch bonnet pepper
½ teaspoon / 2 mL salt
¼ teaspoon / 1 mL black pepper

IN a medium saucepan over medium heat, melt the butter. Sauté the green onions, onions, tomato, and mushrooms until the vegetables are tender. Stir in the coconut milk. Boil for 10 to 15 minutes or until nicely thickened.

STIR in the carrots; cook for 2 to 3 minutes. Add the celery, broccoli, green beans, thyme, Scotch bonnet pepper, salt, and black pepper. Simmer until the vegetables are cooked yet still crunchy. If the sauce is too thick, add 1 to 2 tablespoons / 15 to 25 mL water. Remove the thyme sprigs before serving.

EGGPLANT CASSEROLE

SINCE CHRISTOPHER COLUMBUS'S ARRIVAL IN 1493, THE SPANISH HAVE INTRODUCED MANY FOODS TO JAMAICA'S CUISINE, AMONG THEM CILANTRO, CHICKPEAS, ONIONS, GARLIC, AND EGGPLANT. YOUR FAMILY (ESPECIALLY THE KIDS) AND FRIENDS WILL LOVE THIS EGGPLANT DISH, EVEN IF THEY ARE UNAWARE OF ITS NUTRITIONAL VALUE.

Preparation and cooking time: 1 hour

Yield: 3–4 servings

2 eggplants (about 3 pounds / 1.5 kg)
½ teaspoon / 2 mL salt
1 (16-ounce / 454-mL) can whole tomatoes
2 tablespoons / 25 mL butter
1 onion, sliced (about 1 cup / 250 mL)

¼ cup / 60 mL seasoned dry bread crumbs
2 tablespoons / 25 mL ketchup
1 teaspoon / 5 mL hot pepper sauce (optional)
½ teaspoon / 2 mL black pepper
1 cup / 250 mL shredded cheddar cheese

CUT the eggplant into slices or wedges. Place it in a colander and sprinkle with the salt. Allow it to drain for 20 minutes.

MEANWHILE, preheat the oven to 350°F / 180°C. Lightly grease 2 baking sheets.

RINSE the eggplant thoroughly and towel dry. Arrange the eggplant on the baking sheets. Bake until the eggplant is dry. Set aside. Do not turn off the oven.

DRAIN the tomatoes, reserving the juices; coarsely chop the tomatoes. Melt the butter in a medium saucepan over medium heat. Sauté the onion and tomatoes until the onions are limp. Stir in the bread crumbs, ketchup, hot pepper sauce, black pepper, and the juice from the tomatoes. Simmer for 3 minutes. Remove from the heat.

IN a casserole dish, layer the eggplant and the tomato mixture. Top with the cheese. Bake for 15 to 20 minutes or until hot and the cheese is melted.

VEGETABLE CASSEROLE

YOU WILL ENJOY THE SEASONINGS, HEARTY CONSISTENCY, AND TASTE OF THIS DISH EVEN IF YOU ARE NOT A VEGETARIAN. AFTER TRYING THIS RECIPE, YOU WILL NOT BE ABLE TO THINK OF A BETTER WAY TO USE UP YOUR LEFTOVER RICE AND VEGETABLES.

Preparation and cooking time: 1½ hours

Yield: 6–8 servings

6 potatoes, peeled and thinly sliced
  (about 3 pounds / 1.5 kg)
1 turnip, thinly sliced (about ½ pound / 250 g)
1 large onion, sliced
1 cup / 250 mL sliced mushrooms
1 cup / 250 mL cooked pigeon peas
1 cup / 250 mL cooked brown rice

¼ teaspoon / 1 mL minced Scotch bonnet pepper
5 green onions, chopped (about 1 cup / 250 mL)
1 (5.5-ounce / 156-mL) can tomato paste
1 teaspoon / 5 mL salt
¼ teaspoon / 1 mL black pepper
4 cups / 1 L stock of your choice
1 tablespoon / 15 mL butter or margarine

PREHEAT the oven to 350°F / 180°C. Grease a large casserole dish.

IN a large bowl toss together the potatoes, turnip, onion, mushrooms, and pigeon peas. Evenly alternate layers of vegetables and thin layers of cooked rice in the casserole dish, ending with a layer of vegetables. Sprinkle with the Scotch bonnet pepper and green onions.

STIR the tomato paste, salt, and black pepper into the stock and pour the mixture over the casserole. Dot with the butter.

COVER and bake for 30 to 45 minutes or until the vegetables are cooked through. Serve hot.

POTATO BALLS

THIS IS JUST ONE OF MANY SNACKS JAMAICAN MOTHERS PREPARE FOR THEIR CHILDREN THROUGHOUT THE YEAR.

Preparation and cooking time: 45 minutes to 1 hour

Yield: 10–12 balls

2 cups / 500 mL mashed potatoes (about 3 potatoes)
2 tablespoons / 25 mL butter, melted
½ teaspoon / 2 mL salt
¼ teaspoon / 1 mL black pepper
¼ teaspoon / 1 mL celery salt
¼ teaspoon / 1 mL cayenne

1 green onion, finely chopped (about ¼ cup / 60 mL)
1 sprig of parsley, finely chopped
  (about 2 tablespoons / 25 mL)
All-purpose flour for coating
2 cups / 500 mL vegetable oil

IN a bowl combine the mashed potatoes, butter, salt, pepper, celery salt, cayenne, green onion, and parsley; mix together well. Divide the mixture into 10 to 12 equal portions and roll each portion into a ball with your hands. Roll each ball in the flour to lightly coat.

IN a deep medium skillet over medium heat, heat the oil until hot but not smoking. Fry the balls in batches, turning once, until golden brown all over, about 3 to 5 minutes. Drain on paper towels.

SERVE hot with your favorite dip or alone.

CHEESE AND POTATO BALLS

SERVE THESE POTATO BALLS ON THEIR OWN OR WITH YOUR FAVORITE DIP. YOU CAN ALSO SERVE THEM AS A SIDE DISH WITH A SAUCY MEAT OR FISH DISH.

Preparation and cooking time: 45 minutes to 1 hour

Yield: 20–24 balls

4 cups / 1 L mashed potatoes (about 6 potatoes)
1 small onion, grated (about ½ cup / 125 mL)
3 green onions, chopped (about ¾ cup / 275 mL)
4 eggs, hard-boiled and finely chopped
½ cup / 125 mL shredded cheddar cheese
½ cup / 125 mL butter or margarine, melted
1 teaspoon / 5 mL salt
½ teaspoon / 2 mL black pepper

½ teaspoon / 2 mL finely chopped Scotch bonnet pepper
    or hot pepper sauce
½ teaspoon / 2 mL gera (optional)
¼ teaspoon / 1 mL dried thyme
2 eggs
¼ cup / 60 mL milk
2 cups / 250 mL dry bread crumbs
2 cups / 500 mL vegetable oil

IN a bowl combine the mashed potatoes, onion, green onions, hard-boiled eggs, cheese, butter, salt, black pepper, Scotch bonnet pepper, gera, and thyme; mix well.

IN a shallow dish, whisk the 2 eggs with the milk. Put the bread crumbs in a separate shallow dish.

USING a tablespoon, scoop out 20 to 24 equal portions of the mixture and roll each portion into a ball with your hands. Dip the balls into the egg wash and coat with bread crumbs.

IN a deep medium skillet over medium heat, heat the oil until hot but not smoking. Fry the balls in batches, turning once, until golden brown all over, about 3 to 5 minutes. Drain on paper towels.

SERVE hot.

CALLALOO AND POTATO CROQUETTES

AS IT IS ON MANY CARIBBEAN ISLANDS, CALLALOO IS A SIGNATURE STAPLE OF JAMAICAN CUISINE. ONCE IT'S COOKED, THIS LEAFY GREEN SHRUB HAS THE SAME TEXTURE AS SPINACH WITH A SLIGHTLY MORE DISTINCT TASTE.

Preparation and cooking time: 45 minutes to 1 hour   **Yield: 6–8 croquettes**

2 tablespoons / 25 mL butter
1 green onion, finely chopped (about ¼ cup / 60 mL)
¼ cup / 60 mL finely chopped cooked callaloo
   (about 1 cup / 250 mL uncooked)
½ teaspoon / 2 mL salt
¼ teaspoon / 1 mL black pepper

¼ teaspoon / 1 mL minced Scotch bonnet pepper
¼ cup / 60 mL coconut milk
2 cups / 500 mL mashed potatoes (about 3 potatoes)
1 tablespoon / 15 mL all-purpose flour
1 cup / 250 mL dry bread crumbs
2 cups / 500 mL vegetable oil

IN a large saucepan over medium heat, melt the butter. Sauté the green onion, callaloo, salt, black pepper, and Scotch bonnet pepper until the onions are limp. Stir in the coconut milk and cook for 10 minutes, stirring constantly. Let cool to room temperature.

STIR in the mashed potatoes, and then fold in the flour. Divide the mixture into 6 to 8 equal portions and roll each portion in the palms of your hands to form a cone shape with a rounded peak. Coat the croquettes with bread crumbs. Shake off any excess bread crumbs.

IN a deep medium skillet over medium heat, heat the oil until hot but not smoking. Fry the balls in batches, turning once, until golden brown all over, about 3 to 5 minutes. Drain on paper towels.

SERVE hot.

SIDE DISHES

~~~~~~~~~~~

"IF FISH CUM FROM
RIVA BATTAM AN TELL YUH
SHE SHARK DUNG DEH,
DEN SHARK DUNG DEH"

He who feels it, knows it.

PLAIN ROTI (CHAPATIS)

MY MOTHER TAUGHT ME HOW TO MAKE "JAMAICAN BAKES," A THICKER VERSION OF ROTI MADE BY JAMAICANS OF AFRICAN DESCENT. IT WASN'T UNTIL I BECAME A RESTAURATEUR IN OTTAWA THAT I WAS TAUGHT HOW TO MAKE REAL ROTI — THE TYPE MADE BY THE INDIAN COMMUNITY IN JAMAICA. THERE ARE VARIOUS TYPES, FOR EXAMPLE "BUS-UP SHUT" (BURST-UP SHIRT) ROTI — THE COOKED ROTI RESEMBLES LAYERS OF TORN FABRIC.

Preparation and cooking time: 30 to 45 minutes   **Yield: 6–10 roti**

2 tablespoons / 25 mL butter
3 cups / 750 mL all-purpose flour
1 tablespoon / 15 mL baking powder

½ teaspoon / 2 mL salt
1 cup / 250 mL water
Vegetable oil

In a mixing bowl cut the butter into the flour until the mixture is crumbly. Stir in the baking powder and salt. Make a well in the center of the flour mixture and pour the water into the well. Using your hands, knead the mixture in the bowl, starting from the center and working outward. When a dough forms, add 1 teaspoon / 5 mL oil and continue to knead until the dough is smooth, about 10 minutes.

Cut the dough into 6 to 10 equal portions (handful sizes). On a lightly floured surface, roll out 1 portion to a circle about the size of a bread plate (about 10 inches / 25 cm). Add about ½ teaspoon / 2 mL oil to the center of the dough. Carefully fold the dough into a ball, making sure the oil does not escape. Flatten the ball between your hands and lightly brush it with oil. Set the dough aside on a cookie sheet and cover with a tea cloth. Repeat with the remaining portions and let them rest, covered, for about 15 minutes.

Roll out each piece of dough into a very thin circle (like a crêpe).

Place a large skillet on medium heat. When it is hot, use a pastry brush to brush a thin layer of oil in the pan. Place 1 roti in the pan and brush it with a thin layer of oil. When the dough starts to bubble, usually within 30 seconds, flip the dough and brush the other side with a thin layer of oil. Once the roti starts to bubble on the second side, flip it again and cook for about 30 seconds or until the roti begins to brown lightly in spots. Put the cooked roti on a plate and keep covered with a tea cloth while you cook the remaining roti.

Serve with your favorite curry dish.

FRIED DUMPLINGS
(JOHNNY CAKES)

FRIED DUMPLINGS ARE A VERY TRADITIONAL DISH IN JAMAICA. THEY ARE OFTEN CONFUSED WITH THE AMERICAN JOHNNYCAKES, BUT THEY ARE DENSER AND MUCH MORE FULL IN THEIR TEXTURE AND TASTE.

Preparation and cooking time: 30 minutes   Yield: 6–10 dumplings

1½ cups / 375 mL all-purpose flour
3 tablespoons / 45 mL butter, cut in pieces
2 teaspoons / 10 mL baking powder

½ teaspoon / 2 mL salt
⅓ cup / 75 mL milk or water
1 cup / 250 mL vegetable oil

IN a mixing bowl, combine the flour, butter, baking powder, and salt. Use your hands to mix the ingredients together. Pour in the milk and knead well until the dough is soft but not sticky. (If the dough is sticky, knead in more flour, about a handful at a time. If the dough is too dry and stiff, gradually knead in milk or water 1 tablespoon / 15 mL at a time.)

CUT the dough into 6 to 10 equal portions. Roll each piece into a ball, and then flatten it so the dumpling is about ½ inch / 1 cm thick.

IN a large skillet over medium-low heat, heat about ¼ inch / 5 mm of the oil until hot but not smoking. Carefully add the dumplings and fry them until they are golden on the bottom. Turn the dumplings and cook the second side until golden. Drain the dumplings on paper towels.

SERVE with ackee and salted codfish (page 39), callaloo and salted codfish (page 41), or stewed meats.

BOILED DUMPLINGS

YOU CAN MAKE YOUR DUMPLINGS ROUND AND FLAT OR YOU CAN ROLL THE DOUGH BETWEEN YOUR PALMS, CREATING LONG SLENDER DUMPLINGS. JAMAICANS CALL THESE DUMPLINGS "SPINNERS," AND WE OFTEN COOK THEM IN SOUPS AND STEWS.

Preparation and cooking time: 30 minutes   **Yield: 4–6 dumplings**

1 cup / 250 mL all-purpose flour
½ teaspoon / 2 mL salt

¼ cup / 60 mL water
1 teaspoon / 5 mL vegetable oil or butter

IN a medium bowl, combine the flour and salt. Add half of the water and knead the mixture with your hands, gradually mixing in the oil and the remaining water until the dough is soft and smooth, not sticky. The longer you knead your dumpling dough, the firmer your boiled dumplings will be. (If the dough is sticky, gradually knead in additional flour, about a handful at a time. If the dough is too dry and stiff, knead in water about 1 teaspoon / 5 mL at a time.)

CUT the dough into 4 to 6 equal portions. Roll each piece into a ball, and then flatten it so the dumpling is about ½ inch / 1 cm thick.

HALF fill a medium saucepan with water. Salt the water and bring it to a rolling boil. Carefully drop the dumplings into the boiling water. (You can also cook the dumplings in a soup or stew.) Boil the dumplings until they are firm and stiff, usually 10 to 15 minutes, or until they begin to float.

PUMPKIN PUDDING

THIS MAY BE USED AS AN ALTERNATIVE TO SWEET POTATOES AT THANKSGIVING OR SERVED AS A SIDE DISH TO A SAVORY PORK DISH AT SUNDAY DINNER.

Preparation and cooking time: 1 to 1½ hours

Yield: 6–8 servings

1 (2-pound / 1-kg) pumpkin
4 eggs
1 cup / 125 mL condensed milk
½ cup / 125 mL all-purpose flour

¼ cup / 60 mL sugar
¼ cup / 60 mL butter
½ teaspoon / 2 mL ground cinnamon

USING a sharp knife, peel the pumpkin. Seed the pumpkin and cut the flesh into small cubes. Place the pumpkin cubes in a large saucepan and cover with water. Salt the water and bring it to a rolling boil. Boil the pumpkin for 20 minutes or until it is tender. Drain and let cool.

PREHEAT the oven to 400°F / 200°C. Generously grease a 2-quart / 2-L casserole dish.

IN a bowl, mash the pumpkin. Add the eggs, condensed milk, flour, sugar, butter, and cinnamon; mix well. Turn the mixture out into the casserole and bake for 45 minutes or until the pudding has a thick relish texture.

SERVE with a main dish or as a dessert topped with whipped cream.

BOILED GREEN BANANAS

BANANAS GROW LIKE WEEDS IN JAMAICA. IN FACT, BOTANISTS SAY THEY ARE A FORM OF GRASS. BANANA VARIETIES RANGE IN SIZE, SHAPE, AND TASTE, AND THERE ARE EVEN DISTINCT DIFFERENCES IN COLOR AND FLAVOR. GREEN BANANAS (BOILING BANANAS) ARE YELLOW BANANAS THAT ARE HARVESTED BEFORE THEY HAVE REACHED THEIR RIPENING STAGE.

Preparation and cooking time: 20 to 30 minutes   **Yield: 4–5 servings**

6 green bananas
2 tablespoons / 25 mL vegetable oil

1 teaspoon / 5 mL salt

THE skin of green bananas is very tough and sometimes stubborn in coming off. The more traditional way of peeling green bananas is to cut off the stem and bottom tip and run the point of a sharp knife lengthwise down the banana to split the skin from top to bottom. Using your thumb, pry the skin away from the banana, and then scrape away what's left of the rough inner coat with the knife blade.

HOWEVER, there is a much easier and quicker way of removing the skin. Using a sharp knife, remove the banana stem and bottom tip. Run the point of the knife lengthwise down the banana to split the skin from top to bottom. Cut the banana in two crosswise. Bring a large pot of water to a boil. Add the oil and salt. Carefully place the bananas in the boiling water. Cover the pot and reduce the heat to medium-high. Cook the bananas until they are soft yet still firm, about 20 minutes. Drain the bananas and let cool. The skins will very easily peel away.

COOKED green bananas are great with any saucy meat or fish dish.

BREADFRUIT STUFFING

A FRIEND ONCE TOLD ME THAT HER HUSBAND MADE THE BEST CHESTNUT STUFFING FOR THEIR CHRISTMAS TURKEY. AFTER TASTING IT, I DID AGREE IT WAS WONDERFUL. THEN I THOUGHT HOW SIMILAR THE TASTE OF CHESTNUT IS TO BREADFRUIT, AND SOON I WAS IN MY KITCHEN EXPERIMENTING WITH THIS FLAVORFUL HOLIDAY-SEASON RECIPE. MY FRIEND TELLS ME HER FAMILY NOW HAS *TWO* CHERISHED STUFFINGS FOR THEIR CHRISTMAS DINNER.

Preparation and cooking time: 1½ to 2 hours   Yield: Stuffing for 1 large bird

4 cloves garlic
Turkey liver, neck, and gizzard
¾ cup / 175 mL water
½ cup / 125 mL seasoned dry bread crumbs
¼ cup / 60 mL butter
1 tomato, chopped (about 1½ cups / 375 mL)
1 large onion, finely chopped
   (about 1½ cups / 375 mL)

1 stalk celery, finely chopped (about 1¼ cups / 325 mL)
2 green onions, chopped (about ½ cup / 125 mL)
1 teaspoon / 5 mL salt
1 teaspoon / 5 mL black pepper
1 teaspoon / 5 mL dried thyme
1 teaspoon / 5 mL garlic powder
2 cups / 500 mL cubed cooked breadfruit (page 40)

CRUSH 3 of the garlic cloves; set aside. Put the remaining garlic clove in a medium saucepan with the turkey liver, neck, and gizzard and salt to taste. Add water to cover, then bring to a boil. Boil until the turkey pieces are tender. Let cool.

REMOVE the meat from the turkey neck and cut the meat, gizzard, and liver into small pieces; set aside. (You may also want to keep the liquid for making gravy.)

IN a small bowl stir the water into the bread crumbs; set aside.

IN a medium skillet over medium heat, melt the butter. Sauté the tomato, onion, celery, green onions, crushed garlic, salt, pepper, thyme, and garlic powder until the onions are limp. Stir in the soaked bread crumbs, breadfruit, and cut-up meat. Cover and simmer for 5 minutes. Allow the stuffing to cool before stuffing the bird.

MUSHROOM STUFFING

THiS STUFFING MAY BE USED WITH FISH, POULTRY, OR VEGETABLES (TRY SQUASH, TOMATOES, OR GREEN PEPPERS). YOU CAN ALSO SERVE IT AS A SIDE DISH WITH A MEAT OR FISH DISH.

Preparation and cooking time: 30 minutes　　　　　　　　　　　　**Yield: 3–4 servings**

½ cup / 125 mL water or stock of your choice
½ cup / 125 mL dry bread crumbs
2 tablespoons / 25 mL butter or vegetable oil
1 small onion, finely chopped (about ½ cup / 125 mL)
1 green onion, finely chopped (about ¼ cup / 60 mL)

1 cup / 250 mL chopped mushrooms
½ teaspoon / 2 mL dried thyme
½ teaspoon / 2 mL salt
¼ teaspoon / 1 mL black pepper
Finely chopped hot pepper to taste

In a small bowl stir ¼ cup / 60 mL of the water into the bread crumbs; set aside.

In a medium saucepan over medium heat, melt the butter. Sauté the onion, green onion, and mushrooms until the onions are limp. Stir in the bread crumbs, thyme, salt, black pepper, and hot pepper. Simmer for 2 to 3 minutes; the stuffing should not be watery.

CALLALOO STUFFING

CALLALOO IS A GREEN LEAF SHRUB FOUND ALL OVER THE CARIBBEAN. FOR DECADES MANY WOMEN IN JAMAICA HAVE MADE THEIR LIVING BY GROWING CALLALOO. EVEN TODAY, THROUGHOUT MANY URBAN AND RURAL DISTRICTS, WOMEN CAN STILL BE HEARD SHOUTING, "FRESH CALLALOO, GREEN CALLALOO!" IN THE EARLY-MORNING HOURS. THIS STUFFING IS TASTY WITH FOWL OR FISH, OR INSIDE GREEN PEPPERS OR TOMATOES.

Preparation and cooking time: 20 to 30 minutes   Yield: 3 cups / 750 mL

2 tablespoons / 25 mL vegetable oil
1 small onion, chopped (about ½ cup / 125 mL)
2 cloves garlic, chopped (about 1 tablespoon / 15 mL)
1 small tomato, diced (about ½ cup / 125 mL)
½ teaspoon / 2 mL finely chopped Scotch bonnet
    pepper (optional)

1 teaspoon / 5 mL garlic powder
½ teaspoon / 2 mL salt
¼ teaspoon / 1 mL black pepper
2 cups / 500 mL cooked callaloo, chopped

IN a medium skillet over medium heat, heat the oil. Sauté the onion, garlic, tomato, and Scotch bonnet pepper until the onions are limp. Stir in the garlic powder, salt, and black pepper. Fold in the callaloo, reduce the heat to low, and simmer, covered, until the callaloo is tender, about 10 minutes. Let cool before using.

JAMAICAN RICE AND PEAS

JAMAICA'S COAT OF ARMS, GRANTED IN 1661, SHOWS A MALE AND FEMALE ARAWAK STANDING ON EACH SIDE OF A SHIELD THAT HAS A RED CROSS WITH FIVE GOLDEN PINEAPPLES LINING IT. ON TOP OF THE CREST STANDS A CROCODILE ATOP A ROYAL HELMET. BUT IF YOU WERE TO ASK ANY JAMAICAN, "WHAT IS THE MOST POPULAR COAT OF ARMS?" I GUARANTEE YOU THEY WILL REPLY, "RICE AND PEAS."

Preparation and cooking time: 45 minutes to 1 hour   Yield: 4–6 servings

1 (19-ounce / 540-mL) can gungo peas (pigeon peas) or kidney beans
2 cups / 500 mL coconut milk
2 green onions, chopped (about ½ cup / 125 mL)
1 whole hot pepper

½ teaspoon / 2 mL dried thyme
½ teaspoon / 2 mL salt
½ teaspoon / 2 mL black pepper
2 cups / 500 mL rice
1 tablespoon / 15 mL margarine

IN a large measuring cup, combine the liquid from the canned peas with the coconut milk. Add more water if necessary to make 3½ cups / 875 mL of liquid. Pour the liquid into a large saucepan and add the peas, green onions, hot pepper, thyme, salt, and black pepper. Bring to a rolling boil and boil for 3 minutes. Add the rice and margarine; stir the pot once. (Don't burst the pepper.) Reduce the heat to low, cover, and simmer for 20 to 30 minutes or until the water has completely evaporated and the rice is cooked. (If the rice is not tender after the water evaporates, add 2 to 4 tablespoons / 25 to 50 mL of water, cover, and simmer for another 5 to 10 minutes.) Serve hot.

JAMAICAN TURN CORNMEAL (AFRICAN UGALI)

JAMAICANS ONCE TERMED THIS DISH "THE POOR MAN'S FOOD." SHOULD A FRIEND DROP IN WHILE THIS WAS BEING PREPARED OR SERVED, IT WOULD BE HIDDEN AND THE USUAL COURTESY OF A DINNER INVITATION WOULD NOT BE EXTENDED. THAT ATTITUDE HAS SINCE CHANGED. YOU WILL LOVE THIS DISH WITH SOME WELL-SPICED FISH OR MEAT. TURN CORNMEAL IS ALSO GOOD FOR REDUCING YOUR CHOLESTEROL COUNT.

Preparation and cooking time: 30 minutes

Yield: 3–4 servings

1 cup / 250 mL cornmeal
1 cup / 250 mL milk
1 cup / 250 mL coconut milk or water

¼ teaspoon / 1 mL salt
2 tablespoons / 25 mL butter

IN a large saucepan combine the cornmeal, milk, coconut milk, and salt. Stir with a fork until there are no lumps. Place the pot on medium heat and cook, stirring frequently, until the mixture starts to bubble. Immediately reduce the heat to low and cook, stirring constantly, for about 10 minutes, until the liquid dries out and the mixture has the consistency of mashed potatoes.

ADD the butter, stirring the mixture once more, and cover. Simmer on low heat for 15 minutes to cook the cornmeal completely. When the mixture starts to pull away from the sides of the pot, stir it, then turn it out onto a slightly wet pie plate. Smooth the cornmeal and let it cool.

CUT into wedges and serve.

SWEET POTATO RELISH

THIS IS ONE OF MY FAVORITE DISHES FOR MANY REASONS: IT'S SIMPLE TO PREPARE, IT ALWAYS GETS RECIPE REQUESTS FROM GUESTS, AND ITS SWEET, SMOOTH FLAVOR COMPLEMENTS ANY SAVORY DISH. I RECOMMEND YOU ADD THIS DISH TO YOUR NEXT CHRISTMAS OR THANKSGIVING TURKEY DINNER. THIS DISH IS GOOD WITH PORK OR POULTRY.

Preparation and cooking time: 1 to 1½ hours   Yield: 6–7 servings

4 cups / 1 L peeled and cubed sweet potatoes or Mexican yams (about 4 small potatoes)
½ cup / 125 mL all-purpose flour
⅓ cup / 75 mL brown sugar
¼ cup / 60 mL milk

2 tablespoons / 25 mL margarine
½ teaspoon / 2 mL salt
½ teaspoon / 2 mL ground cinnamon
1 egg, well beaten
¼ teaspoon / 1 mL ground nutmeg (optional)

HALF fill a large saucepan with water. Bring to a rolling boil. Add the potatoes and boil until they are tender.

MEANWHILE, preheat the oven to 350°F / 180°C. Generously grease a 2-quart / 2-L casserole dish or baking dish.

DRAIN the potatoes and, in a large bowl, mash them with the flour, sugar, milk, margarine, salt, and cinnamon. Blend in the egg and nutmeg. Pour the batter into the casserole dish and bake for 45 to 60 minutes or until the top is nicely brown. Let cool.

CUT into squares before serving.

GREEN BANANA CHIPS

THE NEXT TIME YOU ARE ENTERTAINING, PREPARE THESE BANANA CHIPS FOR YOUR GUESTS. IT WILL DELIGHT THEIR TASTE BUDS AND SPARK A GOOD CONVERSATION.

Preparation and cooking time: 45 minutes to 1 hour　　　　　　**Yield: 6–8 servings**

6 green bananas, peeled (page 88)　　　　　　1 cup / 250 mL vegetable oil
1 tablespoon / 15 mL salt

SLICE the green bananas lengthwise or into rounds. Fill a large bowl with water and stir in the salt until dissolved. Add the bananas and let stand for 15 minutes. Drain the bananas and towel dry.

POUR ¼ inch / 5 mm oil into a large skillet and heat the oil over medium-low heat until hot but not smoking. Working in batches, carefully add the banana slices and fry, turning once, until they are golden brown. Drain the banana chips on paper towels and sprinkle with more salt if desired.

SERVE hot or cold. These chips are great with Avocado Cream Cheese Dip (page 134).

COCONUT CHIPS

I DEVELOPED THIS RECIPE WHEN MY CHILDREN WERE GROWING UP AND I WAS LOOKING FOR NEW WAYS TO EXCITE THEIR PALATES. YOU CAN ALSO SERVE THESE CHIPS AS FINGER FOODS WITH SLIVERS OF AVOCADO.

Preparation and cooking time: 30 to 45 minutes

Yield: 12–15 chips

¾ cup / 375 mL grated fresh coconut (1 small coconut)
½ cup / 125 mL milk
2 tablespoons / 25 mL margarine

1½ cups / 375 mL all-purpose flour
½ teaspoon / 2 mL baking powder

PREHEAT the oven to 350°F / 180°C.

SPREAD the coconut on a baking sheet and bake, stirring often, until golden, about 10 minutes. Let cool. Do not turn off the oven.

COMBINE the milk and margarine in a saucepan and heat over low heat, stirring, just long enough to melt the margarine. Let cool.

BLEND the flour and baking powder in a mixing bowl. Add the cooled milk mixture and the coconut; stir until smooth.

GREASE a cookie sheet. Turn the dough out onto a floured surface and roll it thinly. Cut the dough into 2-inch / 5-cm fingers or rounds and transfer them to the cookie sheet. Prick the dough with a fork.

BAKE the chips until light brown, 15 to 20 minutes. Cool on a rack and store in an airtight container.

SERVE with dip.

BEVERAGES

~~~~~~~~~~~~~~~

"MI COME YA FI DRINK
MILK, MI NUH COME
YA FI COUNT COW"

Attend to business at hand
and don't interfere in other
people's matters.

PINEAPPLE LEMONADE

THE PINEAPPLE IS SAID TO BE NATIVE TO PARAGUAY AND SOUTHERN BRAZIL, WHERE IT GROWS WILD, AND THE NATIVE INDIANS BROUGHT THE FRUIT TO THE WEST INDIES BEFORE COLUMBUS ARRIVED IN 1493. COLUMBUS TOOK PINEAPPLES BACK TO SPAIN WITH HIM, AND THEY WERE EVENTUALLY SPREAD AROUND THE WORLD VIA SAILING SHIPS — THE CREWS REPORTEDLY ATE PINEAPPLE TO PROTECT THEMSELVES FROM SCURVY.

Preparation and cooking time: 20 to 30 minutes (plus chilling time)   Yield: 3–4 cups / 750 mL–1 L

1 cup / 250 mL water
1 cup / 250 mL sugar
1 teaspoon / 5 mL ground ginger

2 cups / 500 mL crushed pineapple
¼ cup /60 mL lemon juice
2 cups / 500 mL ice water

IN a medium saucepan bring the water to a boil. Stir in the sugar and ginger. Boil for another 15 minutes, stirring occasionally. Remove the pot from the heat and stir in the pineapple and lemon juice. Let cool.

STRAIN the mixture to remove any pulp. Stir in the ice water. Chill before serving.

PINEAPPLE SUMMER QUENCHER

CHRISTOPHER COLUMBUS FIRST DOCUMENTED PINEAPPLES ON HIS SECOND VOYAGE TO THE CARIBBEAN ISLANDS, IN 1493. HOWEVER, THE INDIANS OF SOUTH AMERICA, MEXICO, AND THE WEST INDIES WERE ENJOYING THE FRUIT LONG BEFORE THEN!

Preparation time: 30 minutes (not including sitting time)   Yield: 4 cups / 1 L

1 pineapple
5-inch /12-cm piece fresh ginger, finely chopped
   (about ½ cup / 125 mL)
2 limes, chopped with skin

4 cups / 1 L boiling water
2 cups / 500 mL sugar (or to taste)
¼ cup / 60 mL lemon juice

WASH the pineapple thoroughly in cold water. With a sharp knife remove the pineapple's stem and leaves; discard. Cut the pineapple into large chunks, and in a food processor finely chop the pineapple with its skin. Transfer the pineapple to a large nonreactive sealable container. Stir in the ginger and limes. Pour the boiling water over the mixture, stir once, and cover tightly. Let stand for 24 hours in a cool room.

STRAIN the liquid to remove any pulp. Stir in the sugar and lemon juice until the sugar is dissolved. Serve over cracked ice.

TROPICAL JULEP

THIS MAY BE YOUR ONLY LEGITIMATE EXCUSE TO USE THOSE FANCY DRINK UMBRELLAS YOU'VE BEEN SAVING. YOU MAY ALSO WANT TO GARNISH THE RIM OF EACH GLASS WITH A WEDGE OF ORANGE AND ADD A PINEAPPLE CHUNK AND CHERRY ON A TOOTHPICK.

Preparation time: 20 to 30 minutes (includes chilling time)　　　　**Yield: 3 cups / 750 mL**

2½ cups / 625 mL orange or grapefruit juice
¼ teaspoon / 1 mL salt

1 cup / 250 mL sweetened condensed milk
½ teaspoon / 2 mL ground nutmeg

IN a large pitcher, stir together the orange juice and salt. Chill for 15 minutes. Add the condensed milk and nutmeg. Stir well and serve over cracked ice.

PAPAW JULEP

UNLESS YOU HAVE A FAVORITE FLAVOR YOU NEVER STRAY FROM, I SUGGEST YOU USE VANILLA ICE CREAM WITH THIS RECIPE. THE VANILLA COMPLEMENTS AND BALANCES THE WILD TROPICAL AROMA AND TASTE OF THE PAPAW.

Preparation time: 20 to 30 minutes   Yield: 3–4 cups / 750 mL–1 L

2 cups / 500 mL puréed papaw
1½ cups / 375 mL evaporated milk
¾ cup / 175 mL sugar

1 cup / 250 mL ice cream (flavor of your choice)
1 teaspoon / 5 mL angostura bitters
½ teaspoon / 2 mL vanilla

In a blender, or in a large bowl with a whisk, blend the papaw, evaporated milk, and sugar. Blend in ½ cup / 125 mL of the ice cream, the bitters, and vanilla. Serve in chilled glasses topped with scoops of the remaining ice cream.

PAPAW AND ORANGE JULEP PUNCH

PAPAW IS ALSO COMMONLY KNOWN AS PAPAYA. IT HAS A CREAMY CUSTARD-LIKE FLESH THAT IS BEST DESCRIBED AS A COMBINATION OF TROPICAL FRUIT FLAVORS. IT'S LIKE TASTING A MANGO AND BANANA WITH A LITTLE PINEAPPLE, ALL IN THE SAME MOUTHFUL.

Preparation time: 20 to 30 minutes (plus chilling time)   Yield: 2–3 cups / 500–750 mL

2 cups / 500 mL puréed papaw
1 cup / 250 mL sugar (or less to taste)
1 cup / 250 mL orange juice

¼ cup / 60 mL grenadine
2 teaspoons / 10 mL lime juice
1½ cups / 375 mL ginger ale (optional)

IN a blender, or in a large bowl with a whisk, blend the papaw, sugar, orange juice, grenadine, and lime juice. Chill. When ready to serve, stir in the ginger ale and pour into chilled glasses.

TEA PUNCH

THIS IS A GREAT DRINK TO KICK OFF ANY OCCASION, BE IT A BACKYARD BARBECUE OR A HOLIDAY SEASON PARTY.

Preparation and cooking time: 20 to 30 minutes (plus chilling time)   **Yield: 12–14 cups / 3–3.5 L**

1½ cups / 375 mL sugar
1 cup / 250 mL water
3 cups / 750 mL orange juice
2 cups / 500 mL strawberry syrup
1½ cups / 375 mL ice tea mix

1 cup / 250 mL grapefruit juice
1 cup / 250 mL pineapple juice
1 cup / 250 mL lemon juice
2 cups / 500 mL 7Up

IN a small saucepan over medium heat, bring the sugar and water to a boil, stirring; boil, stirring occasionally, for 5 minutes or until the liquid thickens to a syrup. Let cool.

IN a punch bowl, stir together the orange juice, strawberry syrup, ice tea mix, grapefruit juice, pineapple juice, lemon juice, and sugar syrup. Chill.

JUST before serving, stir in the 7Up.

TROPICAL FRUIT PUNCH

FOR AN ATTRACTIVE PRESENTATION, POUR THE PUNCH INTO A BOWL ON A LARGE ROUND GLASS PLATTER. DECORATE THE PLATTER WITH TROPICAL FLOWERS AND FERNS OR FRUITS AND FLOWERS. JUST BEFORE SERVING, GARNISH THE PUNCH WITH THIN SLICES OF CITRUS AND CHERRIES.

Preparation time: 10 to 15 minutes　　　　　　　**Yield: 12–14 cups / 3–3.5 L**

3 cups / 750 mL orange juice
1 cup / 250 mL honey
1 cup / 250 mL cocktail mix
¼ cup / 60 mL sugar
¼ cup / 60 mL lime juice

4 cups / 1 L 7Up
4 cups / 1 L purple grape juice
3 cups / 750 mL pineapple juice
Rum to taste (optional)

IN a punch bowl, combine the orange juice, honey, cocktail mix, sugar, and lime juice. Stir until the sugar and honey dissolve. Stir in the 7Up, grape juice, and pineapple juice. Add desired amount of ice cubes. Add the rum and stir once.

MANGO PUNCH

MANGOES HAVE BEEN CULTIVATED FOR NEARLY 4,000 YEARS IN MANY WARM-CLIMATE COUNTRIES AROUND THE WORLD. ANCIENT TRAVELERS USED TO DESCRIBE THEM AS THE WORLD'S MOST DELICIOUS FRUIT.

Preparation and cooking time: 30 to 45 minutes   Yield: 6 cups / 1.5 L

¼ cup / 60 mL water
¼ cup / 60 mL sugar
3 cups / 750 mL mango juice

2 cups / 500 mL orange juice
1 cup / 250 mL pineapple juice
1 tablespoon / 15 mL lime juice

In a small saucepan, bring the water and sugar to a boil; boil for 10 minutes, stirring constantly. Let the syrup cool.

In a large bowl stir together the sugar syrup, mango juice, orange juice, pineapple juice, and lime juice. Chill.

Serve over crushed ice.

PUMPKIN PUNCH

I CAME UP WITH THIS RECIPE ONE FALL MANY YEARS AGO WHEN WE HAD MORE PUMPKINS THAN WE KNEW WHAT TO DO WITH. A FRIEND CHALLENGED ME TO CREATE A TASTY PUMPKIN BEVERAGE. I SUCCEEDED, AS YOU WILL SOON FIND OUT.

Preparation and cooking time: 20 to 30 minutes (plus chilling time)　　　Yield: 12–13 cups / 3–3.25 L

1 (2-pound / 1-kg) pumpkin, peeled and finely chopped
4 cups / 1 L water
1 teaspoon / 5 mL salt
3 cups / 750 mL orange juice
1 cup / 250 mL sugar (or to taste)

1 cup / 250 mL honey or grenadine
2 teaspoons / 10 mL lime juice
¼ cup / 60 mL cherry brandy (optional)
1 teaspoon / 5 mL angostura bitters

IN a large saucepan simmer the pumpkin, water, and salt over medium heat until the pumpkin is tender. Remove the pot from the heat and let cool. Do not drain the pumpkin.

IN a blender purée the pumpkin, in batches if necessary. In a large pitcher, stir together the pumpkin, orange juice, sugar, honey, and lime juice until the sugar is dissolved. Chill.

JUST before serving, stir in the brandy and bitters. Serve in chilled glasses.

BANANA SHAKE

MY FATHER USED TO CULTIVATE BANANAS FOR EXPORT TO THE U.K. UNFORTUNATELY, THERE WERE TIMES WHEN THE MARKET WAS SATURATED, AND BANANA SHIPMENTS DID NOT LEAVE THE PORT. SOMETIMES MY FATHER WOULD HAVE AS MUCH AS A FREIGHT CAR FULL OF RIPE BANANAS, AND NOT EVEN THE FLIES COULD EAT ALL OF THEM. SO WE WERE OFTEN LEFT WITH A LOT OF BANANAS TO USE AS CREATIVELY AS POSSIBLE.

Preparation time: 5 minutes　　　　　　　　　　　　**Yield: 5–6 cups / 1.25–1.5 L**

4 well-ripened bananas, peeled
3 cups / 750 mL evaporated milk
¾ cup / 175 mL sugar (or to taste)

½ teaspoon / 2 mL vanilla
½ teaspoon / 2 mL ground nutmeg
3 scoops ice cream (flavor of your choice)

IN a blender, combine the bananas, evaporated milk, sugar, vanilla, nutmeg, and ice cream. Blend until smooth. Serve immediately.

GUAVA SHAKE

IT'S BELIEVED THAT GUAVA ORIGINATED IN SOUTHERN MEXICO AND WAS EVENTUALLY SPREAD BY BIRDS OR MAN TO THE WEST INDIES SOMETIME IN THE MID-SIXTEENTH CENTURY. JAMAICANS PRIMARILY USE GUAVA FOR DRINKS AND DESSERTS, OR AS A REFRESHING SNACK FOR CHILDREN. IF YOU ARE FEELING FESTIVE, ADD A SPLASH OF JAMAICAN APPLETON RUM.

Preparation time: 5 minutes   **Yield: 3–4 cups / 750 mL–1 L**

3 cups / 750 mL cold milk   ½ cup / 125 mL sugar (or to taste)
1½ cups / 375 mL guava juice

IN a blender, blend the milk, guava juice, and sugar. Serve over crushed ice.

RUM SOUR

RUM IS DISTILLED FROM FERMENTED SUGARCANE, MOLASSES, OR CANE SYRUP. SUGARCANE IS NOT NATIVE TO THE CARIBBEAN. THE SPANISH EXPLORERS BROUGHT IT ON THEIR JOURNEYS, AND COLUMBUS WAS SAID TO HAVE PLANTED SUGARCANE ON HIS SECOND VOYAGE TO THE ISLANDS, THUS INTRODUCING IT TO THE JAMAICAN ARAWAKS. THIS WAS JUST BEFORE THE DISCOVERY THAT RUM COULD BE MADE FROM FERMENTED CANE JUICE.

Preparation and cooking time: 2 minutes   Yield: 1 serving

¼ cup / 60 mL amber rum
1 tablespoon / 15 mL lemon juice
1 teaspoon / 5 mL sugar

¼ teaspoon / 1 mL lemon bitter*
½ slice orange for garnish
1 maraschino cherry for garnish

*Lemon bitter can be found in the beverages and cocktail section of most supermarkets.

PUT the rum, lemon juice, sugar, and lemon bitter in a shaker with cracked ice. Shake well. Pour into a chilled glass. Garnish with the orange slice and cherry.

MILD RUM PUNCH

RUM PUNCH IS TO JAMAICANS WHAT APPLE PIE IS TO NORTH AMERICANS; COMPETITIONS FOR THE BEST RECIPES ARE FIERCE. AND ALTHOUGH I'VE NEVER WON AN OFFICIAL BLUE RIBBON, THIS RECIPE HAS WON THE PRAISES OF ALL THOSE WHO HAVE TASTED IT — EVEN BEFORE THE SECOND AND THIRD GLASS!

Preparation time: 5 minutes   Yield: 1 serving

⅓ cup / 75 mL amber rum
2 tablespoons / 25 mL lime juice

1 tablespoon / 15 mL grenadine or honey
½ teaspoon / 2 mL angostura bitters

Mix together the rum, lime juice, grenadine, and bitters. Pour the drink over cracked ice in a chilled glass and serve immediately.

SUMMER COOLER

THIS DRINK HOLDS FOND CHILDHOOD MEMORIES FOR ME. THIS WAS A THURSDAY-EVENING DRINK FOR US EVERY TWO WEEKS. ON HIS WAY HOME MY DAD WOULD PICK UP THE INGREDIENTS AND PREPARE THIS DRINK — MINUS THE RUM — FOR US CHILDREN. RUM WOULD BE ADDED WHENEVER HE SERVED THE ADULTS.

Preparation time: 2 minutes

Yield: 5–6 cups / 1.25–1.5 L

4 cups / 1 L cola
2 cups / 500 mL vanilla ice cream

½ cup / 125 mL amber rum
Maraschino cherries for garnish

PUT the cola, ice cream, and rum in a blender. Blend until smooth and foamy. Serve in tall glasses over crushed ice, topped with cherries.

BEER PUNCH

THIS DRINK IS IDEAL FOR WINTER NIGHTS. YOU CAN USE ANY KIND OF BEER, AND ANY BRAND OF AMBER RUM, ALTHOUGH JAMAICAN APPLETON RUM MAKES A MORE AUTHENTIC DRINK.

Preparation and cooking time: 30 to 45 minutes

Yield: 4–5 cups / 1–1.25 L

4½ cups / 1.25 L beer
1 tablespoon / 15 mL ground ginger
½ teaspoon / 2 mL ground nutmeg

4 eggs
½ cup / 125 mL brown sugar
½ cup / 125 mL amber rum

IN a large saucepan over medium heat, heat 4 cups / 1 L of the beer. (Keep the remaining beer cold.) Remove the beer from heat and let it stand for 10 minutes. Stir in the ginger and nutmeg.

IN a blender, blend the eggs for a few seconds. Add the cold beer and sugar; pulse to blend. With the motor running, slowly add the heated beer mixture until well blended. Blend in the rum. Serve immediately.

GUINNESS STOUT PUNCH

IN JAMAICA THIS DRINK IS TRADITIONALLY PREPARED FOR THE MAN OF THE HOUSE ON SUNDAY MORNINGS. IT IS SAID TO ENHANCE THE VIRILITY OF ANY MAN WHO DRINKS IT.

Preparation time: 5 minutes   Yield: 3 cups / 750 mL

1 egg
½ cup / 125 mL evaporated milk
2 tablespoons / 25 mL sugar
¼ teaspoon / 1 mL ground nutmeg

¼ teaspoon / 1 mL vanilla
1 bottle Guinness stout
2 tablespoons / 25 mL amber rum (optional)
4 ice cubes

IN a blender, or in a bowl using an electric mixer, beat the egg until it is foamy. Blend in the milk, sugar, nutmeg, and vanilla, beating until the sugar dissolves. Stir in the stout, rum, and ice. Mix well and serve immediately.

BANANA RUM SHAKE

I WAS RAISED ON A FARM WITH LOTS OF BANANA, COCONUT, AND BREADFRUIT TREES. MY MOTHER ALWAYS TRIED TO MAKE THE BEST USE OF THE OVER-RIPE PRODUCE THAT COULD NOT BE TAKEN TO MARKET, AND BANANA SHAKES WERE A TREAT MOM WOULD MAKE FOR US CHILDREN ONCE IN A WHILE. AS I GOT OLDER, I DISCOVERED THAT A SPLASH OF RUM TURNED A CHILDHOOD FAVORITE INTO A DELIGHTFUL ADULT TREAT.

Preparation time: 5 minutes

Yield: 7–8 cups / 1.75–2 L

4 well-ripened bananas, peeled
3 cups / 750 mL evaporated milk
1 cup / 250 mL sugar (or to taste)
½ teaspoon / 2 mL ground nutmeg

½ teaspoon / 2 mL vanilla
3 scoops ice cream (flavor of your choice)
⅓ cup / 75 mL amber rum
½ teaspoon / 2 mL almond extract

IN a blender, blend together the bananas, evaporated milk, sugar, nutmeg, and vanilla until smooth. Add the ice cream, rum, and almond extract; blend until smooth. Serve immediately in chilled glasses.

DESSERTS

~~~~~~~~~~

"YUH NUH DUN YET"

You are not finished.

TROPICAL FRUIT SALAD

THIS WAS ONE OF MY CHILDREN'S FAVORITE DESSERTS. I DIDN'T MIND MAKING IT OFTEN BECAUSE IT WAS SO EASY TO PREPARE. IF YOU MAKE THIS RECIPE FOR YOUR FAMILY, MAKE SURE YOU TELL THEM HOW HARD YOU WORKED TO PREPARE IT. BELIEVE ME, THE TASTE WILL MAKE THEM THINK YOU WORKED ALL DAY!

Preparation time: 10 minutes (not including chilling time)   Yield: 4–5 servings

8 ounces / 250 g cream cheese
½ cup / 125 mL confectioners' sugar
½ teaspoon / 2 mL vanilla

2 cups / 500 mL Dream Whip
1 (14-ounce / 398-mL) can tropical fruit cocktail, drained
Graham cracker crumbs for topping

IN a medium bowl, cut the cream cheese into small cubes. Add the confectioners' sugar and vanilla; cream together. Fold the Dream Whip into the cream cheese mixture. Fold in the fruit cocktail. Turn the mixture into a glass bowl and smooth the top. Sprinkle with the graham cracker crumbs. Refrigerate for at least 30 minutes.

SPOON into individual serving bowls.

FRIED RIPE PLANTAINS

ALMOST EVERY JAMAICAN PREPARES PLANTAINS, AND THIS IS THE MOST COMMON RIPE PLANTAIN RECIPE. ALTHOUGH PLANTAINS ARE IN THE BANANA FAMILY, UNLIKE BANANAS THEY ARE NEVER EATEN RAW. WHEN THEY ARE GREEN, THEY ARE PREPARED IN STEWS OR FRIED AS CHIPS (SEE PAGE 95). AND WHEN THEY ARE RIPENED AND BROWN, AND THEIR STARCH CONTENT HAS TURNED TO SUGAR, THEY ARE DELICIOUS AS A SWEET DESSERT.

Preparation and cooking time: 15 minutes　　　　　　　　　　**Yield: 2–3 servings**

1 ripe plantain　　　　　　　　　　2 tablespoons / 25 mL canola oil

PEEL the plantain and cut on an angle into 1-inch / 2.5-cm chunks.

HEAT a medium skillet over medium heat. When it is hot, add the oil. When the oil is hot but not smoking, carefully add the plantain slices; reduce the heat to low. Fry the plantains until they are golden brown on the bottom, about 3 minutes. Turn and fry until the other side is golden brown. Drain the plantains on paper towels. Serve hot, drizzled with some rum sauce (page 140).

GRAPEFRUIT SNAPS

GRAPEFRUIT GROWN IN JAMAICA IS THE SAME KIND AS THOSE GROWN IN NORTH AMERICA, BUT I'VE ALWAYS FOUND THE JAMAICAN GRAPEFRUIT TO BE MUCH SWEETER. I THINK THIS IS BECAUSE OF THE SOIL AND TEMPERATURE IN WHICH THEY ARE GROWN.

Preparation time: 30 minutes   Yield: 3–4 cups / 750 mL–1 L

2 grapefruits
2 seedless oranges
½ teaspoon / 2 mL angostura bitters

½ cup / 125 mL brown sugar (or to taste)
1 tablespoon / 15 mL amber rum
Maraschino cherries for garnish

CUT the grapefruits in half. Using a grapefruit knife, cut grapefruit sections from the membranes and the peel. Spoon sections into a large bowl. Remove any seeds. Peel the oranges and cut away all the white membranes. Cut the oranges into chunks and add to the grapefruit. Add the bitters and mix well. Sprinkle with sugar; pour the rum over all.

SERVE in dessert glasses topped with cherries.

COCONUT DROPS

iN Jamaica, coconut drops are sold as treats during recess and lunch periods at many elementary school gates.

Preparation and cooking time: 1 to 1½ hours

Meat from 2 medium coconuts, cut into pea-sized pieces
Sugar, enough to equal amount of coconut

1 cup / 250 mL water
¼ cup / 125 mL finely chopped fresh ginger

In a large measuring cup, measure the coconut. Measure out an equal amount of sugar. Have ready a cookie sheet or sheets of waxed paper.

In a medium saucepan combine the coconut, sugar, water, and ginger. Over medium heat and without stirring, boil until the water evaporates. Begin stirring, and cook, stirring frequently, until the sugar thickens and caramelizes. Be careful not to burn the caramel. The liquid should be thick and not runny. (To test whether the mixture is ready, drop a small spoonful into a glass of cold water. If it hardens, then it is ready.) Remove from the heat.

Drop the mixture by tablespoons / 15 mL onto waxed paper or a cookie sheet. Cool the drops to room temperature before serving.

GINGER CANDY

WE ALWAYS HAD EXCESS PRODUCE AND SPICES ON OUR FARM IN JAMAICA, SO YOU CAN IMAGINE THE NUMBER OF EXPERIMENTAL DISHES — ESPECIALLY THE ONES WE CHILDREN TRIED — THAT WOULD RESULT IN FAILURES AND UPSET STOMACHS. HENCE THE ORIGIN OF GINGER CANDY. GINGER CANDY NOT ONLY TASTES GREAT BUT GINGER HELPS YOUR DIGESTION.

Preparation and cooking time: 1 to 1½ hours

Yield: 6–8 servings

¾ cup / 175 mL milk
2 cups / 500 mL white sugar
1 cup / 250 mL brown sugar
2 tablespoons / 25 mL corn syrup

3 tablespoons / 45 mL butter
½ pound / 250 g ginger, finely chopped or grated
1 teaspoon / 5 mL vanilla

HAVE ready a greased cookie sheet.

IN a medium saucepan bring the milk to a boil. Immediately remove from the heat and stir in the white sugar, brown sugar, and corn syrup. Place the pot over low heat and cook, stirring frequently, until the mixture begins to thicken. Remove from the heat and drop in the butter. Don't stir in the butter. Let cool slightly.

IN a blender, blend the mixture until it thickens. Stir in the ginger and vanilla. Pour the mixture onto the cookie sheet and cut into desired serving pieces before it cools.

SWEET POTATO DUCKUNOO

LIKE SO MANY OF JAMAICA'S TRADITIONAL DISHES, THIS EXOTIC TREAT CAME ABOUT THROUGH THE CONVERGENCE OF CULTURES ON THE ISLAND, NAMELY CHINESE AND SPANISH. ALTHOUGH DUCKUNOO IS USUALLY SERVED AS A SNACK, IT CAN BE SERVED ALONGSIDE SOME STEAMED VEGETABLES AND A SPICY DISH LIKE BROWN STEW PORK (PAGE 66).

Preparation and cooking time: 1 hour

Yield: 12–14 servings

4 cups / 1 L grated peeled sweet potato
   (about 4 small potatoes)
1 cup / 250 mL grated peeled yellow yam
   (about ½ pound / 250 g)
2 cups / 500 mL all-purpose flour
2 cups / 500 mL brown sugar
1 cup / 250 mL coconut milk

½ cup / 125 mL evaporated milk
¾ teaspoon / 3 mL salt
2 teaspoons / 10 mL margarine or butter, melted
1 teaspoon / 5 mL vanilla
½ teaspoon / 2 mL ground nutmeg
½ cup / 125 mL raisins

PLACE the sweet potatoes, yam, and flour in a large bowl and mix well. In a medium bowl, combine the brown sugar, coconut milk, evaporated milk, and salt. Stir until the sugar dissolves. Stir in the margarine. vanilla, and nutmeg. Add the coconut mixture to the sweet potato mixture and stir until well combined, soft, and creamy. Stir in the raisins.

SCOOP about ¼ cup / 60 mL of the mixture onto 12 to 14 6-inch /15-cm squares of waxed paper. Fold the corners up to make a 2-inch / 5-cm parcel and tie the parcel with a piece of string.

HALF fill a large saucepan with lightly salted water and over medium-high heat bring to a rolling boil. Carefully submerge the parcels in the boiling water and cook for 40 minutes.

SERVE alone as a snack or as a dessert with rum sauce (page 140).

SWEET POTATO PUDDING (JAMAICAN PONE)

MY MOTHER HANDED DOWN THIS RECIPE TO ME JUST AS HER MOTHER HAD HANDED IT DOWN TO HER. JAMAICAN PONE IS ONE OF THE OLDEST TRADITIONAL DESSERTS ON THE ISLAND, WITH AS MANY VARIATIONS TO THE RECIPE AS THERE ARE JAMAICANS.

Preparation and cooking time: 1 to 1½ hours

Yield: 8–10 servings

2 pounds / 1 kg sweet potatoes (4 to 5 potatoes)
2½ cups / 625 mL coconut milk
2 cups / 500 mL all-purpose flour
1½ cups / 375 mL brown sugar
1 cup / 250 mL raisins or currants

¼ cup / 60 mL margarine or butter, melted
2 teaspoons / 10 mL vanilla
1 teaspoon / 5 mL salt
1 teaspoon / 5 mL ground nutmeg
½ teaspoon / 2 mL ground cinnamon

PREHEAT the oven to 300°F / 150°C. Grease a 9-inch / 23-cm square baking dish.

PEEL and grate the sweet potatoes. In a large bowl, combine the potatoes, coconut milk, flour, sugar, raisins, margarine, vanilla, salt, nutmeg, and cinnamon; mix well. Pour the mixture into the baking dish and bake for 45 to 60 minutes or until the liquid is absorbed and the top of the pone is golden brown.

COOL before serving. This is great with rum sauce (page 140).

GUAVA CUSTARD

WHEN I WAS A CHILD, GUAVA WAS ONE OF MY FAVORITE FRUITS TO WORK WITH WHILE EXPERIMENTING IN THE KITCHEN. I EVENTUALLY PERFECTED A GUAVA JELLY THAT I SOLD TO MY NEIGHBORS AND SCHOOL FRIENDS. AS I GOT OLDER THE EXPERIMENTING CONTINUED, UNTIL I PERFECTED THIS CUSTARD RECIPE.

Preparation and cooking time: 30 minutes   **Yield: 4–5 servings**

1 cup / 250 mL milk
½ teaspoon / 2 mL ground nutmeg
½ teaspoon / 2 mL vanilla
¼ cup / 60 mL butter, softened

1 cup / 250 mL sugar
4 eggs
1 cup / 250 mL crushed guava

IN a medium saucepan, combine the milk, nutmeg, and vanilla. Heat over medium heat just until bubbles form. Set aside.

IN a medium bowl, cream the butter. Gradually beat in the sugar. Beat in the eggs one at a time. Slowly beat in the scalded milk.

RETURN the mixture to the saucepan and cook over medium-low heat for 5 to 10 minutes, stirring frequently. Do not let boil. Stir in the guava and continue to cook for another 5 minutes. Do not let boil.

POUR into individual custard cups. Chill, uncovered, before serving.

PLANTAIN PUDDING

THIS DISH WAS CREATED BY ONE OF OUR FARM HANDS IN JAMAICA. WE HAD AN ABUNDANCE OF PLANTAINS AND SOMETIMES THERE WOULD NOT BE A MARKET FOR ALL THAT WE HARVESTED. THIS MEANT VARIOUS DISHES WERE CREATED, AND SOME WERE BETTER THAN OTHERS. THIS IS WITHOUT A DOUBT ONE OF THE BEST.

SERVE THIS PUDDING HOT WITH YOUR FAVORITE MEAT DISH OR AS A DESSERT.

Preparation and cooking time: 1½ hours   Yield: 12–15 servings

8 well-ripened plantains
1 teaspoon / 5 mL salt
1 tablespoon / 15 mL lime juice
4 eggs
1 cup / 250 mL sweetened condensed milk

½ cup / 125 mL all-purpose flour
¼ cup / 60 mL sugar
¼ cup / 60 mL butter, melted
1 teaspoon / 5 mL vanilla
½ teaspoon / 2 mL ground nutmeg

CUT the plantains in half crosswise. Put the plantains in a large pot and add the salt and enough water to cover. Bring to a boil and cook for 20 minutes or until the skins start to separate from the plantains. Drain the plantains. When they are cool enough to handle, remove and discard the skins.

PREHEAT the oven to 350°F / 180°C. Generously grease a 10-inch / 25-cm square baking dish.

IN a blender or food processor, blend the plantains until they are mushy. Add the lime juice and blend briefly. Add the eggs, condensed milk, flour, sugar, butter, vanilla, and nutmeg. Blend well.

TURN the mixture out into the baking dish and bake for 50 minutes or until the pudding is firm.

CUT into squares and serve hot.

BAKED BREAD PUDDING

I HAVE TASTED MANY BREAD PUDDINGS, BUT WHEN I WAS SERVED THIS ONE AT A FRIEND'S DINNER PARTY I PRACTICALLY BEGGED HER FOR THE RECIPE. SHE TOLD ME THAT IT WAS HER GRANDMOTHER'S DISH. SHE NOT ONLY GAVE THE RECIPE TO ME BUT IS HAPPY TO PASS IT ON TO YOU.

Preparation and cooking time: 1½ hours

Yield: 6–7 servings

4 cups / 1 L milk, warmed
1½ cups / 375 mL sugar
¼ cup / 60 mL butter, melted
2 teaspoons / 10 mL vanilla
1 teaspoon / 5 mL ground nutmeg

½ teaspoon / 2 mL salt
6 eggs, beaten
15 to 20 cherries, pitted and quartered
½ cup / 125 mL raisins
10 slices dry bread, cubed (about 4 cups / 1 L)

IN a medium bowl, combine the milk, sugar, butter, vanilla, nutmeg, and salt; mix well. Add the beaten eggs, cherries, and raisins; mix well. Add the bread and mix well. Set aside for 30 minutes.

MEANWHILE, preheat the oven to 325°F / 160°C. Butter a 3-quart / 3-L casserole or baking dish.

POUR the bread mixture into the casserole dish and bake for 50 to 60 minutes or until a knife inserted into the center of the pudding comes out clean.

SERVE warm or cold.

ORANGE PEACH CAKE

THIS IS A VERY LIGHT AND DELICIOUS CAKE. WHEN IT'S BAKED, THE TOP IS GOLDEN. AS YOU CUT INTO IT, THE INSIDE IS AS BRIGHT AS THE HOT JAMAICAN SUN!

Preparation and cooking time: 1¼ hours   Yield: 6–8 servings

3 cups / 750 mL all-purpose flour
1 tablespoon / 15 mL baking powder
½ pound / 250 g butter, softened
⅔ cup / 150 mL sugar

4 eggs
1 teaspoon / 5 mL vanilla
½ cup / 125 mL orange juice
½ cup / 125 mL peach nectar

PREHEAT the oven to 350°F / 180°C. Set oven racks on the lowest shelf and the top shelf. Grease a 9-inch / 23-cm cake pan.

IN a bowl stir together the flour and baking powder.

IN a medium bowl, cream the butter and sugar. Beat in the eggs one at a time. Beat in the vanilla. Continue beating while adding the orange juice and peach nectar. Fold in the flour mixture.

TURN the batter into the cake pan and bake on the lowest shelf for 35 minutes. Move the cake to the top shelf and bake for 5 minutes or until browned on top and a knife inserted in the center comes out clean. Cool the cake in the pan and then turn out onto a rack.

JAMAICAN EASTER BUN

THIS TRADITIONAL TREAT IS PREPARED BY JAMAICANS FOR THE EASTER HOLIDAY. THIS DARK BUN IS DENSE IN TEXTURE AND RICH IN TASTE. IT IS BEST SERVED AT ROOM TEMPERATURE ACCOMPANIED BY A PIECE OF CHEDDAR CHEESE. MOST JAMAICAN KIDS LOOK FORWARD TO EASTER JUST FOR THESE BUNS. ANY OTHER FOOD IS SECONDARY.

Preparation and cooking time: 2 hours   Yield: 1 loaf

2½ cups / 625 mL all-purpose flour
½ cup / 125 mL margarine
1½ cups / 375 mL brown sugar
½ cup / 125 mL currants
½ cup / 125 mL raisins
½ cup / 125 mL citrus peel

2 eggs
½ cup / 125 mL milk
1 teaspoon / 5 mL baking powder
½ teaspoon / 2 mL ground nutmeg
6 whole maraschino cherries

PREHEAT the oven to 350°F / 180°C. Grease a 10-inch / 25-cm square baking pan.

IN a large bowl, add the flour and margarine. Using a pastry cutter or two knives, cut in the margarine until the mixture is crumbly. Stir in the brown sugar, currants, raisins, and citrus peel.

IN a small bowl, beat the eggs. Add the milk; mix well. Pour the milk mixture into the flour mixture; mix well. Stir in the baking powder and nutmeg. Pour the batter into the pan and arrange the cherries on top.

BAKE for 10 minutes. Reduce the heat to 300°F / 150°C and bake for 1 hour and 15 minutes or until a butter knife inserted in the center of the bun comes out clean.

STEAMED CHRISTMAS PUDDING

THE MOST CRUCIAL INGREDIENT TO THIS RECIPE IS THE SOAKED FRUIT. SOAKED FRUIT IS A CONSTANT IN ALL BAKERS' PANTRIES IN JAMAICA. SOME WILL EVEN BE SOAKING THEIR FRUIT FOR CHRISTMAS BAKING AS EARLY AS JULY. TALK ABOUT YOUR POTENT PUDDING!

Preparation and cooking time: 3 hours   Yield: 10–12 servings

Soaked Fruits:
2 cups / 500 mL raisins
1 cup / 250 mL currants
1 cup / 250 mL prunes
1 (750-mL) bottle sweet red wine

¼ cup / 60 mL white rum
2 teaspoons / 10 mL vanilla
1 teaspoon / 5 mL ground nutmeg

Pudding:
1 cup / 250 mL salted butter (½ pound / 250 g)
1 cup / 250 mL dark brown sugar
5 eggs, beaten
4 cups / 1 L soaked fruits
¼ cup / 60 mL finely chopped maraschino cherries
2 tablespoons / 25 mL browning sauce

1 tablespoon / 15 mL rosewater
2 teaspoons / 10 mL almond extract
1¾ cups / 425 mL all-purpose flour
1 teaspoon / 5 mL ground nutmeg
1 teaspoon / 5 mL cinnamon
1 teaspoon / 5 mL baking powder

MAKE the soaked fruits: Wash and pat dry the fruits. Working in batches, coarsely chop the raisins, currants, and prunes in a food processor. Place the chopped fruits in a nonmetallic storage container with a tight lid; add wine, rum, vanilla, and nutmeg. Stir well. Cover and store at room temperature until ready to use.

MAKE the pudding: Grease a 12-inch / 30-cm round baking pan. In a large pot, add enough water to come one-quarter up the sides of the baking pan. Bring water to a boil.

IN a mixing bowl cream the butter and sugar until light and fluffy. Gradually beat in the beaten eggs until well blended. Add the soaked fruits, cherries, browning sauce, rosewater, and almond extract; mix well.

IN another bowl, sift together the flour, nutmeg, cinnamon, and baking powder. Fold the flour mixture into the batter until well combined.

STEAMED CHRISTMAS PUDDING

(CONTINUED)

~~~~~~

TURN the batter out into the steaming pan. Tightly cover with a lid or wax paper tied with string. Set the pan in the water bath and steam for 2½ hours. Remove the pan from the water and let cool.

SERVE with rum sauce (page 140).

IF you prefer to bake this pudding, turn the batter into a greased 12-inch / 25-cm round baking pan and bake uncovered in a 250°F / 120°C oven for 2 hours.

BANANA FRITTERS

TRY POURING THE BATTER OUT IN THE SHAPE OF MEDALLIONS (SILVER DOLLARS) THE NEXT TIME YOU ARE PREPARING THEM FOR A DINNER PARTY. DON'T FORGET TO DRIZZLE A LITTLE RUM SAUCE (PAGE 140) OVER THEM JUST BEFORE SERVING.

Preparation and cooking time: 45 minutes   **Yield: 8–10 fritters**

2 well-ripened bananas
1 egg, beaten
½ cup / 125 mL all-purpose flour
¼ cup / 60 mL milk
2 tablespoons / 25 mL sugar

1 teaspoon / 5 mL vanilla
¼ teaspoon / 1 mL salt
1 cup / 250 mL (approx.) vegetable oil
Confectioners' sugar for garnish

IN a medium bowl, mash the bananas. Stir in the beaten egg, flour, milk, sugar, vanilla, and salt; mix well. The batter should have the consistency of pancake batter. (If the batter is too thick, add about 1 tablespoon / 15 mL milk. If the batter is too thin, add about 2 tablespoons / 25 mL flour.)

IN a large deep skillet over medium-low heat, heat about ¼ inch / 5 mm oil until hot but not smoking. Working in batches, carefully drop the batter by the tablespoonful into the oil. Cook the fritters 2 minutes or until they are brown on the bottom. Turn and cook until the other side is brown, another 2 minutes. Drain the fritters on paper towels.

SERVE hot, sprinkled with the confectioners' sugar.

SWEET POTATO AND BANANA FRITTERS

THIS IS A SPIN-OFF FROM THE BANANA FRITTERS RECIPE. THIS TREAT ORIGINATED WITH ONE OF THE FARM HANDS ON OUR FARM IN JAMAICA.

Preparation and cooking time: 45 minutes

Yield: 12–15 fritters

1 large well-ripened banana, mashed
2 cups / 500 mL mashed cooked sweet potato
2 eggs, beaten
¼ cup / 60 mL all-purpose flour
¼ cup / 60 mL milk
2 tablespoons / 25 mL butter, melted

½ teaspoon / 2 mL salt
½ teaspoon / 2 mL ground cinnamon
½ teaspoon / 2 mL ground nutmeg
½ teaspoon / 2 mL lime juice
1 cup / 250 mL (approx.) vegetable oil
Confectioners' sugar for dusting

IN a medium bowl, combine the banana, sweet potato, eggs, flour, milk, butter, salt, cinnamon, nutmeg, and lime juice; mix well.

IN a large deep skillet over medium-low heat, heat ¼ inch / 5 mm oil until hot but not smoking. Working in batches, carefully drop the batter by the tablespoonful into the oil, keeping the fritters apart. Cook the fritters for 2 minutes or until they are brown on the bottom. Turn and cook until the other side is brown, another 2 minutes. Drain the fritters on paper towels.

SERVE hot, sprinkled with the confectioners' sugar.

PLANTAIN PIE

PLANTAIN PIE IS ONE OF THOSE WONDERFUL DISHES THAT MAKE PEOPLE REALIZE THERE ARE SO MANY POSSIBILITIES TO COOKING. IT TOOK ME SEVERAL YEARS (AND FAILURES) TO COME UP WITH THIS RECIPE, AND I GUARANTEE YOU IT WILL RIVAL THE BEST PUMPKIN PIE YOU HAVE EVER EATEN. SERVE IT AS A DESSERT WITH YOUR NEXT THANKSGIVING OR CHRISTMAS MEAL.

Preparation and cooking time: 1½ hours

Yield: 4–6 servings

3 well-ripened plantains, boiled and puréed (see page 88)
2 eggs, beaten
1½ cups / 375 mL evaporated milk
½ cup / 125 mL brown sugar
3 tablespoons / 45 mL butter, melted

1 teaspoon / 5 mL ground nutmeg
1 teaspoon / 5 mL vanilla
½ teaspoon / 2 mL lime juice
1 (9-inch / 23-cm) unbaked deep pie shell

PREHEAT the oven to 425°F / 220°C.

IN a large bowl, combine the plantains, eggs, evaporated milk, sugar, butter, nutmeg, vanilla, and lime juice; mix well. Pour the mixture into the pie shell and bake for 10 minutes. Reduce the heat to 300°F / 150°C and bake for 45 minutes or until a knife inserted in the center comes out clean.

SERVE warm with a dollop of whipped cream.

SAUCES & DIPS

~~~~~~~~~~~~~~~~

"YUH CAAN PUT NEW WINE IN A OLE BAKLE"

Never put new wine
in a bottle with old wine.

AVOCADO CREAM CHEESE DIP

SLICED AVOCADOS ARE AS COMMON ON JAMAICAN TABLES AT MEALTIME AS BUTTER IS IN NORTH AMERICA. CHILDREN IN JAMAICA GROW UP ON AVOCADOS AS THEY OFFER A HIGHER LEVEL OF ENERGY THAN MOST FRUIT. IN FACT, THE AVOCADO HAS BEEN HONORED IN THE *GUINNESS BOOK OF WORLD RECORDS* AS THE MOST NUTRITIOUS FRUIT.

Preparation time: 30 minutes   Yield: 1½ cups / 375 mL

1 avocado
6 ounces / 175 g cream cheese, softened
2 tablespoons / 25 mL milk
1 tablespoon / 15 mL lemon or lime juice

1 teaspoon / 5 mL grated onion
½ teaspoon / 2 mL white pepper (optional)
¼ teaspoon / 1 mL salt

CUT the avocado in half lengthwise. Remove the seed and scoop the pulp into a small mixing bowl, keeping the peels intact. Mash the pulp. Add the cream cheese, milk, lemon juice, onion, white pepper, and salt; mix well. Spoon the mixture into the avocado peels and serve immediately.

SERVE with potato chips, toast, breadfruit fingers, banana chips (page 95), or crackers.

MANGO CHUTNEY

THIS IS AN OLD-TIME FAVORITE THROUGHOUT THE WEST INDIES, AND ALTHOUGH THERE ARE MANY DIFFERENT RECIPES, I AM CERTAIN YOU WILL ENJOY THIS VERSION, WHICH HAS A LITTLE SPICY KICK THAT ACCENTUATES THE MANGO FLAVOR.

Preparation and cooking time: 2½ hours   **Yield: 14 cups / 3.5 L**

8 cups / 2 L chopped mango
4 cups / 1 L brown sugar
4 cups / 1 L white vinegar
3 cups / 750 mL raisins, chopped

¼ cup / 60 mL minced fresh ginger
2 teaspoons / 10 mL salt
¼ teaspoon / 1 mL minced Scotch bonnet pepper
4 large cloves garlic, chopped (about 2 tablespoons / 25 mL)

IN a stockpot combine the mango, sugar, vinegar, raisins, ginger, salt, Scotch bonnet pepper, and garlic. Cover and bring to a boil without stirring. Immediately reduce the heat to low and begin stirring, making sure the ingredients do not stick to the bottom of the pot. Simmer, covered, for 1½ to 2 hours, stirring occasionally, until desired thickness. Let cool, then bottle chutney in preserving jars. Keep refrigerated.

PEANUT SAUCE

THIS SAUCE IS GREAT WITH JUST ABOUT ALL FRIED FOODS OR COOKED VEGETABLES. TRY IT ON PILI PILI CHICKEN (PAGE 71), POTATO BALLS (PAGE 79), OR ON ESCOVITCH FISH (PAGE 49).

Preparation and cooking time: 20 minutes   **Yield: about 2 cups / 500 mL**

1 small green pepper, finely chopped
  (about 1 cup / 250 mL)
2 cloves garlic, finely chopped
  (about 1 tablespoon / 15 mL)
½ cup / 125 mL smooth peanut butter
½ cup / 125 mL milk

½ cup / 125 mL stock of your choice
1 teaspoon / 5 mL sugar
1 teaspoon / 5 mL soy sauce
½ teaspoon / 2 mL salt
¼ teaspoon / 1 mL black pepper
½ teaspoon / 2 mL hot pepper sauce (optional)

IN a medium saucepan, stir together the green pepper, garlic, peanut butter, milk, stock, sugar, soy sauce, salt, black pepper, and hot pepper sauce. Cook over low heat, stirring frequently, until the sauce thickens, about 5 minutes.

SERVE hot.

RICH BROWN SAUCE

THIS SAUCE IS LISTED AS AN INGREDIENT OF THE FRESH CORN AND BEEF STEW (PAGE 64). BUT GET CREATIVE AND POUR IT OVER OTHER DISHES SUCH AS ANY OF THE JERKS OR FISH RECIPES.

Preparation and cooking time: 10 to 15 minutes   Yield: 1 cup / 250 mL

3 tablespoons / 45 mL all-purpose flour
2 tablespoons / 25 mL margarine
1 cup / 250 mL milk
1 tablespoon / 15 mL soy sauce

1 teaspoon / 5 mL ketchup
½ teaspoon / 2 mL salt
½ teaspoon / 2 mL hot pepper sauce

PLACE the flour and margarine in a medium saucepan. Cook over medium-high heat, stirring constantly, until the mixture is brown. Reduce the heat to low and stir in the milk, soy sauce, ketchup, salt, and hot pepper sauce. Simmer, stirring frequently, until the sauce thickens.

TASTY BROWN SAUCE

THERE ARE NUMEROUS BRANDS OF HOT SAUCES IN JAMAICA, WHICH ISN'T SURPRISING SEEING THAT ALMOST EVERY DISH IN THE CARIBBEAN IS PREPARED WITH A DASH OF HOT PEPPER SAUCE OR HOT PEPPERS. THE TWO MOST POPULAR CARIBBEAN HOT SAUCES THAT CAN BE EASILY FOUND IN GROCERY STORES WORLDWIDE ARE THE RED "PICK-A-PEPPER" FROM JAMAICA AND "MATOUKS" FROM TRINIDAD.

Preparation and cooking time: 15 minutes   **Yield: 1½ cups / 375 mL**

2 tablespoons / 25 mL butter
1 small onion, sliced
3 tablespoons / 45 mL all-purpose flour
¼ teaspoon / 1 mL salt

¼ teaspoon / 1 mL black pepper
1 cup / 250 mL stock of your choice
2 tablespoons / 25 mL soy sauce
½ teaspoon / 2 mL hot pepper sauce

IN a medium saucepan over medium heat, melt the butter. Sauté the onions until they are limp. Add the flour, salt, and black pepper. Stir until the mixture is well browned. Gradually stir in the stock. Stir in the soy sauce and hot pepper sauce.

INCREASE the heat to high and bring the mixture to a quick boil, stirring. Remove from the heat. Strain through a sieve.

BREAD SAUCE

THIS SAUCE PERFECTLY COMPLEMENTS STEAMED VEGETABLES, FRIED FISH, OR STUFFED BAKED POTATOES. YOU CAN ALSO USE IT IN PLACE OF THE CELERY SOUP IN THE SALTED CODFISH AND SWEET POTATO CASSEROLE (PAGE 46).

Preparation and cooking time: 25 to 30 minutes   **Yield: 3 cups / 750 mL**

2 cups / 500 mL milk
1 small onion
2 cloves garlic, crushed (about 1 tablespoon / 15 mL)

1 cup / 250 mL dry bread crumbs
1 tablespoon / 15 mL butter
3 tablespoons / 45 mL heavy cream

PLACE the milk, whole onion, and garlic in a large saucepan. Over medium-high heat, bring the milk to a boil, stirring frequently. Reduce the heat to low and stir in the bread crumbs and butter. Simmer, stirring frequently, for 15 minutes. Discard the onion and garlic. Place the sauce in a blender, and with the motor running add the cream gradually, blending until smooth.

RUM SAUCE

JAMAICAN Appleton rum will give this sauce a sweeter, and more tropical, flavor. Try it on sweet potato pudding (page 122), plantain pudding (page 124), baked bread pudding (page 125), banana fritters (page 130), sweet potato and banana fritters (page 131), or plantain pie (page 132).

Preparation time: 30 minutes   Yield: 2 cups / 500 mL

2 egg yolks
1 cup / 250 mL confectioners' sugar
¼ cup / 60 mL amber rum

1 cup / 250 mL heavy cream
1 teaspoon / 5 mL vanilla

Beat the egg yolks in a medium bowl. Beat in the confectioners' sugar until the sugar dissolves. Pour in the rum slowly and beat until well blended. Set the mixture aside.

In a large bowl, whip the cream until it is stiff. Fold in the vanilla. Fold the egg mixture into the whipped cream.

SETTING THE SCENE FOR THE PERFECT JAMAICAN MEAL: DÉCOR, MUSIC, AND MENUS

IT'S EASY TO SET THE SCENE FOR A PERFECT JAMAICAN DINING EXPERIENCE WITHOUT BREAKING A SWEAT OR YOUR BUDGET. IN FACT, THERE ARE JUST THREE SIMPLE ELEMENTS YOU CAN WORK ON THAT WILL MAKE ALL THE DIFFERENCE: YOUR TABLECLOTH AND PLACE SETTINGS, SOME SIMPLE DECORATIONS, AND SOME SCENE-SETTING MUSIC.

I can guarantee your guests will be more intrigued with the Jamaican dishes you are serving than with your table settings, but these help set the right atmosphere. Choose bright colors such as vibrant blues, greens, yellows, and reds to complement the Caribbean flavors and help create a festive mood.

Bright-colored candles and tropical fruits will brighten up any dining area. If you decide on a centerpiece for your table, make sure it's not too high, or your guests won't be able to see each other. A candle placed on each side of a floral centerpiece is always elegant.

Even if you're just having a casual, informal meal with good friends, it is important to know how a table is properly set. Place settings consist of plates, glasses, cutlery, napkins, and placemats. Each setting should be 1 inch / 2.5 cm from the edge of the table and directly opposite each other. Leave about 18 inches / 45 cm of elbow room between each setting. Glasses should be placed to the right, at or near the point of the knife. Put utensils 1 inch / 2.5 cm from the edge of the table on either side of the plate in the order in which they will be used, beginning with the outside utensils and moving in toward the plate. Finally, napkins go just to the left of the forks.

If you are setting buffet service from a sideboard or sweet table, use a tablecloth that matches or complements the one you chose for your dining table. You may want to consider any of the following for your serving table: a tiered lazy-daisy server with an arrangement of fruits and tropical flowers; candles; a bowl of water with floating candles and flower or rose petals; or scattered small bowls filled with tropical flowers and fruits. Outlining the serving table with rose or flower petals always looks nice.

Don't forget the music. You can spice up a meal even further with music that creates an authentic Jamaican ambiance. Depending on the "feel" of the occasion, or the direction you want the evening to take, you can choose a selection of soft low-bass reggae or the full-band jump-up sounds of calypso. Or you can arrange a lively mix of the two with music selections from artists such as Shaggy, Beanie man, Sly and Robbie, or some of the older artists — Bob Marley, Byron Lee and the Dragonaires, or Peter Tosh. You really can't go wrong with whatever you choose; my only suggestion is to try to cater to your guests' tastes.

NEW YEAR'S DINNER

In the southern United States and the Caribbean, it is believed that if you eat black-eyed peas on New Year's Day you will have good fortune for the rest of the year.

Tea Punch (spiked) (page 103)
Jamaican Vegetable Patties (cocktails) (page 16)
Jerk Pork Pâté (page 12) and crackers
Kool Salad (page 31) OR Steamed Cabbage (page 75)
Baked Salted Codfish and Black-Eyed Peas (page 45) OR Brown Stew Pork (page 66)
Plantain Pie (page 132)

EASTER DINNER

Mango Punch (page 105)
Jamaican Salted Codfish Patties (page 17) (cocktails)
Spicy Salted Codfish Salad (page 36)
Baked Fish with Mushrooms and Tomato (page 52)
White Rice
Jamaican Easter Bun (page 127) OR Baked Bread Pudding (page 125)

A GREAT SIZZLING SUMMERTIME DINNER

Mango Punch (page 105)
Summer Cooler (page 111)
Papaw and Orange Julep Punch (page 102)
Avocado Salad (page 33)
Salted Codfish Fritters (page 18)
Curry Barbecued Chicken (page 58)
Escovitch Fish (page 49)
Tropical Fruit Salad (page 116)

A BIRTHDAY DINNER

MILD RUM PUNCH (PAGE 110)
PINEAPPLE LEMONADE (PAGE 98)
CALLALOO AND POTATO CROQUETTES (PAGE 81)
JAMAICAN BEEF PATTIES (PAGE 14) (COCKTAILS)
GREEN BANANA CHIPS (PAGE 95) OR YOUR FAVORITE POTATO CHIPS
   WITH AVOCADO CREAM CHEESE DIP (PAGE 134)
KOOL SALAD (PAGE 31)
WHITE RICE
CURRY GOAT (PAGE 55)
ESCOVITCH FISH (PAGE 49)
SWEET POTATO PUDDING (JAMAICAN PONE) (PAGE 122)

SUNDAY BREAKFAST

GRAPEFRUIT SNAPS (PAGE 118)
HOT CHOCOLATE
JUICE OF YOUR CHOICE
CALLALOO AND SALTED CODFISH (PAGE 41)
BOILED GREEN BANANAS (PAGE 88) OR FRIED DUMPLINGS (JOHNNY CAKES) (PAGE 85)
FRIED RIPE PLANTAINS (PAGE 117)
JAMAICAN HARD DOUGH BREAD

SUNDAY DINNER

SPICY CUCUMBER SALAD (PAGE 35)
POTATO BALLS (PAGE 79)
JAMAICAN RICE AND PEAS (PAGE 92)
BOILED GREEN BANANAS (PAGE 88)
JERK CHICKEN (PAGE 70)
BAKED WHOLE FISH WITH CALLALOO STUFFING (PAGE 51)
ORANGE PEACH CAKE (PAGE 126)

THANKSGIVING DINNER
~~~~~~

Fresh Green Bean Salad (page 34)
Avocado Salad (page 33)
Sweet Potato Relish (page 94)
Jamaican Rice and Peas (page 92)
Roast Turkey with Breadfruit Stuffing (page 89)
Baked Chocho (page 74)
Guava Custard (page 123)
Sweet Potato and Banana Fritters (page 131) with Rum Sauce (page 140)

CHRISTMAS DINNER
~~~~~~

Tossed salad
Jamaican Potato Salad (page 30)
Plantain Pudding (page 124)
Jamaican Rice and Peas (page 92)
Curry Goat (page 55)
Jerk Pork (page 67) OR Roast leg of pork with Pork Marinade (page 68)
Tropical Fruit Salad (page 116) OR Steamed Christmas Pudding (page 128)

SATURDAY LUNCH WITH FRIENDS
~~~~~~

Banana Shake (page 107)
Spicy Cucumber Salad (page 35)
Potato Balls (page 79)
Stuffed Breadfruit with Ackee and Salted Codfish (page 40)
Banana Fritters (page 130) with Rum Sauce (page 140)
Ginger Candy (page 120)

FATHER'S DAY MEAL

Pumpkin Punch (page 106) OR Guinness Stout Punch (page 113)
Carrot and Cabbage Salad (page 32)
Vegetable Casserole (page 78)
Escovitch Fish (page 49)
Sweet Potato Duckunoo (page 121) with Rum Sauce (page 140)

SHOPPING SOURCES

~~~~~~

Many of the Jamaican ingredients in this cookbook are available at your local chain super-markets and at West Indies, Asian, Central American, or Mexican grocery stores. Your surest bet is to search out a West Indies market. If you are not sure how to go about finding the West Indies market in your city or town, might I suggest you inquire at a beauty salon that caters to the Caribbean community? Another option is to order your Jamaican ingredients online. Here are a few Internet shopping website addresses that you may wish to try.

D.B. Kenney Fisheries Ltd.   http://www.dbkenneyfisheries.com/
Caribbean Island Imports   http://www.caribimports.com/index.html
Caribbeanshop.com   http://www.caribbeanshop.com/shopping/food/

You may also wish to try the following mail order sources.

Patels. Specialty & Bulk Food Store
2210 Commercial Drive
Vancouver, British Columbia, Canada
V5N 4B5
Phone (604) 255-6729
Fax (604) 255-8151

Caribbean Market
1003 Royal Ave.
New Westminster, British Columbia, Canada
V3M 1K3
Phone (604) 522-9480
Fax (604) 522-9480

C-Brands Tropicals
P.O. Box 700248
Goulds, Florida 33032, U.S.A.
Phone (305) 258-1444
Fax (305) 258-0201

Your final option may be to contact us via our website (see page 152). We would be pleased to hear from you and help make your Jamaican dishes as authentic as possible.

GLOSSARY OF INGREDIENTS

Ackee (Ah-KEE): Ackee is the national fruit of Jamaica. It is a bright red tropical fruit that contains three large black seeds and soft creamy yellow flesh. The creamy flesh is used in the very common dish ackee and salted codfish (page 39).

Avocado (A-voh-CAH-doh): There are several varieties of avocado with glossy green, dark green, or black skin. Jamaicans call the fruit "pears" because of their shape. Most avocados do not change color when ripe, so the best test is to give it a gentle squeeze: if the skin gives way slightly, it's ready to be eaten. Avocados are an excellent source of vitamin E and have a good amount of vitamin C and potassium.

Breadfruit: This fruit grows only in the West Indies and parts of the Pacific region. They are round, 7 to 10 inches / 18 to 25 cm in diameter, and have a rough green skin with a mild-tasting dense yellow flesh. Canned breadfruit can be found at West Indies and Asian grocery stores. Breadfruit will have a sweeter taste if it's left to ripen completely before being cooked. It can be baked, boiled, or fried and is best served with savory saucy dishes.

Callaloo (KA-lah-loo): This green leaf shrub is found in the Caribbean Islands. Canned callaloo can also be found in West Indies stores and most supermarkets. Fresh callaloo is vibrant green and resembles spinach; cooking gets rid of its bitter taste. It may be cooked a number of ways, including baking, stir-frying, and boiling. Like spinach, callaloo's volume reduces considerably as it cooks. You may substitute spinach if callaloo is not available.

Chocho (Choh-choh): This vegetable looks like an oversized pear and has one soft seed surrounded by white flesh and pale green skin. Chocho is widely grown in the West Indies and the southern United States, where it's commonly known as "chayote." Chocho is a member of the squash family and has a mild-flavored flesh. It is a good source of potassium.

Coco (Coh-coh): Children often describe this vegetable as a hairy potato, and it's easy to see why. Under the brown hairy skin a coco is roughly the same size and shape as a regular white potato. In other parts of the world, coco is also called "malanga," "cocoyam," and "Japanese potato." The flour made from coco is said to be one of the most hypoallergenic foods in the world.

Garam masala (GAR-am ma-SAH-lah): In Punjabi, garam means "ground spices." The Western label "masala" is considered broken Punjabi to Indians because the word means "sautéed vegetables." There are numerous variations of the spice blend containing anywhere from two to twelve ground spices. Masala can include black pepper, cloves, coriander, cumin, cardamom, dried chiles, mace, nutmeg, cinnamon, and other spices. You will find garam masala in West Indies and Indian stores and in the spice section of most supermarkets.

Green bananas: These are unripe bananas, picked halfway through the development stages of ripened bananas. Green bananas can be found in West Indies stores.

Green onions: Jamaicans call these "skellions," and some North Americans call them "spring onions."

Guava (GWAH-vah): This tropical fruit has a sweet fragrance, a unique taste, and the texture of a pear. There are many varieties, ranging in size from a small onion to a medium apple and in color from yellow to purple-black. Its soft flesh ranges from pale yellow to bright red. Guava should be very ripe before it is eaten, and it is also sold in cans at many supermarkets. It is a good source of vitamins A and C.

Kidney bean: A firm, medium-sized bean that has dark red skin and cream-colored flesh. It is one of the few beans that is flavorful on its own. Canned or dried kidney beans can be found in supermarkets and grocery stores.

Lima bean (LY-muh): These broad, flat, light-green or cream-colored beans are also called butterbeans. They have a bland taste but soak up flavors. Lima beans are a good source of protein and vitamins A and C.

Mango (MAN-goh): Unbelievably, this fruit belongs to the same family as the cashew nut. Ripe mangoes have a red blush to them, although some varieties do have a greener appearance when ripe. Ripe mangoes yield to a gentle squeeze and emit a distinctive aroma. Ripe mangoes should be stored in the refrigerator. Mangoes are rich in vitamins A, C, and D.

Okra (OH-krah): A long, rigid, fuzzy seedpod that grows to the size of an adult's finger and is dark green. When selecting fresh okra, choose the smaller pods, as larger pods tend to be tougher, and select only firm, blemish-free pods. Although made famous in Caribbean cuisine, okra is also used in Mediterranean and Creole dishes. Okra's gummy juices make it useful as a thickener in soups and stews, but it is more commonly served whole as a vegetable. Okra's flavor is similar to that of eggplant. It is best served when boiled or steamed until tender-crisp to retain its flavor and nutrients. Fresh okra contains vitamins A and C.

Oxtail: Many people make two mistakes when they think of oxtail. The first is to think the cut of meat actually comes from an ox when in fact it comes from a cow. The other mistake is to dismiss oxtail as a bony cut of meat, when it is actually one of the meatiest and most succulent pieces of meat. You can get oxtail from your local butcher or grocer's meat counter. Ask your butcher to cut the oxtail at the joints, making 1-inch / 2.5-cm pieces that are convenient for cooking and eating.

Papaw (PAW-paw): This fruit is also called "papaya" and ranges from 2 to 6 inches / 5 to 15 cm in length. Its skin usually turns yellow as it ripens, although some varieties remain green. Its flesh is pale yellow and lavished with seeds. Once ripe, papaw has a custard-like texture and a succulent, sweet flavor reminiscent of bananas and pears. Papaya is a very good source of vitamins A and C. It may be cut and refrigerated for a short time. Papaya is a seasonal fruit and can be difficult to find at times but is well worth the hunt. Look in West Indies, Indian, or Asian markets, and some supermarkets.

Pigeon peas: Jamaicans call these legumes "gungo peas." Pigeon peas are firm and creamy yellow, and are about the size of garden peas. Canned or dried pigeon peas can be found in supermarkets and in West Indies markets.

Pimento (pi-MEN-toh): More commonly known as allspice, dried pimento seeds are a little smaller than garden peas. Pimento can be found in any West Indies store and at supermarket spice counters. Pimento — actually a berry — grows everywhere in Jamaica and the nearby islands, where most of the world's supply is produced. Allspice was given its name because it tastes like a combination of cinnamon, nutmeg, and cloves. When cooking with whole pimento seeds, be certain to remove the seeds before serving.

Pineapple: Pineapple flesh is fibrous, golden-yellow, and very sweet and juicy. When ripe, its skin takes on a brownish golden tint and the fruit emits a distinctive aroma. The juiciest pineapples are usually large and plump and feel heavy for their size. Don't be intimidated when faced with having to use a fresh pineapple. They are easier than you might think to skin and cut up. First, cut off the top about ½ inch / 1 cm below the crown leaves. Stand the fruit upright on a cutting board and hold it steady with one hand. Using a sharp knife, slice off the skin (usually about ¼ inch / 5 mm thick) from the top to the bottom of the fruit. Turn the fruit as you continue to slice off the skin. Cut out any tough "eyes." Then slice the pineapple in half lengthwise and slice each half in half again. Finally, slice the core from each quarter. Now you can slice or cube and enjoy the pineapple as you wish.

Plantain (PLAN-tane): This fruit is part of the banana family, although typically larger than the common banana. They grow in India, Africa, and South America as well as the West Indies. The fruit is green when young and turns light orange or yellow (or sometimes a combination of both) when ripe. Like green bananas, plantains can be boiled, fried, or baked. They are a good source of potassium and vitamin C.

Pumpkin: Jamaican pumpkins are the same as the pumpkins grown in North America; they are all members of the squash family. However, I suggest you try the pumpkins from a West Indies store. Pumpkins grown in the West Indies tend to have less water, making them firmer and tastier when cooked.

Scotch bonnet pepper: A small chile pepper, usually 1 inch / 2.5 cm in diameter, round and dimpled. They come in various colors, including red, orange, yellow, and green. They are considered the most flavorful and the hottest pepper on the market. Scotch bonnet peppers are used in many recipes in this book. You may substitute other peppers, but you will not find a hotter pepper or one that enhances the taste of spices as nicely as the Scotch bonnet. Be certain to wash your hands after handling a Scotch bonnet pepper or you may inadvertently get the pepper's oils in your eyes.

    Some of my recipes call for whole Scotch bonnet peppers and advise removing the pepper before serving (carefully, so it doesn't burst — remember, the seeds of a pepper are far hotter than the skin and flesh). Cooking a whole pepper in a soup or other dish allows for most of the pepper's flavor to seep into the dish without releasing its full fiery strength. You will know it is time to remove a Scotch bonnet pepper when the skin becomes thin. Other recipes call for finely chopped or minced Scotch bonnet peppers. If you are not accustomed to hot peppers, try adding only half of what the recipe calls for and gradually work your palate up to the resilience of any Jamaican.

Stock: A liquid containing nutrients and flavor extracted from meat, poultry, fish, or vegetables that are cooked over low heat.

Thyme: A herb with hundreds of varieties. Fresh thyme has greenish-gray leaves, which turn a duller green after it is dried. There is a great difference in flavor between fresh thyme and dried thyme. With dried thyme, the leaves have been stripped from the plant, dried, and ground up, and in the process the herb loses a great deal of its potency. This is why I suggest you use fresh thyme whenever possible. Some recipes call for "sprigs of fresh thyme." A sprig is a small branch covered with leaves. Many herb advocates will tell you that thyme has many benefits, such as aiding with digestion of fats and lowering cholesterol levels. However, Jamaicans, and I'm sure many other cultures, use thyme simply for its distinct taste and ability to enhance whatever dish it is cooked in. Fresh thyme can be found at any herb store or West Indies store.

GLOSSARY OF COOKING TERMS

~~~~~~

Baste: To pour pan juices, marinades, or other liquids over foods during cooking to keep food moist.

Broil: To cook food with the heat source directly above it.

Cream: To beat ingredients — usually a fat and sugar — together until light and creamy.

Crush: To break or press into small pieces. Some recipes in this cookbook call for crushed ingredients such as pineapple or guava. Most stores sell these in cans; however, it is easy to crush fruits or vegetables using the largest holes on a hand-held grater. Grate the fruit or vegetable over a bowl, catching all the juices. You can also use a food processor.

Cut in: To work fat into flour by using a dull knife or a pastry blender to cut the fat into small pieces, making it easier to blend with the flour.

Fold: To combine a light ingredient (such as whipped cream) with a heavier ingredient (such as cream cheese). Both ingredients are placed in a bowl and a spatula or wide spoon is used to gently scoop the ingredients on top of each other until they are combined without losing volume.

Grate: To shred fruits, vegetables, or cheese using a hand-held grater or a food processor. Save the juices to use in the recipe unless told to discard.

Grease: To coat a baking pan or other dish with a light film of oil, butter, shortening, or cooking spray to prevent sticking while baking.

Knead: To work a dough with your hands to thoroughly mix flour and other ingredients into a smooth dough.

Marinate: To cover a food with a liquid or paste blend before cooking. A marinade enhances the flavor of meat or fish as well as tenderizing it. You can make your meats that much more tasty and juicy by giving them a three-minute massage with the seasonings.

Roast: To bake meat, fish, or vegetables in an oven, usually without a cover.

Sauté: To cook quickly and lightly in a small amount of fat or low-fat spray, stirring frequently.

Scald: To heat milk or cream to just below the boiling point. The technique is used to slow the souring of milk and also to bring milk to the right temperature for preparing custards and similar foods.

Simmer: To cook slowly in liquid over low heat at just below the boiling point.

SUGAR AND SPICE ONLINE

This book would not have been possible without the encouragement, input, and support of our restaurant customers and friends. As you read and use this cookbook we would like to think of you as new friends, and we invite you to visit our website at: http://members.home.net/everythingirie

Should you have any comments or questions about this book, its recipes, or the ingredients, feel free to e-mail us at everythingirie@home.com.

When you visit *Sugar and Spice and Everything Irie* online, you will find additional recipes, photos of the more exotic ingredients in this book, photos of Jamaica, and more. Do keep in touch, and we promise to do the same. See you there!

— VEDA AND MARRETT

INDEX

INDEX

~~~~~~

casserole, 78
casserole, eggplant, 77
chochos, 147
chocho, baked, 74
coco, 147
coconut vegetables, 76
okra, 148
patties, 16
rundun, 76
soup, 27
soup, beef and vegetable, 25
soup, cream of callaloo, with okra, 24

Y

Yams. *See also* Sweet potato(es)
    oxtail soup I, 20
    soup, beef, 23

ABOUT THE AUTHORS

~~~~~~

Veda Nugent

Since her humble first efforts, at age six, cooking for the family's much-loved pig in Flint River, Jamaica, Veda has prepared traditional island dishes for literally thousands of people.

Veda arrived in Canada from Jamaica in 1972, with two small children, two suitcases, and six hundred dollars, to begin a new life. From 1982 to 1989 she operated two successful Caribbean restaurants in Ottawa, Ontario. As a restaurateur and chef she gained much recognition while introducing the tastes of the islands to the Ottawa Valley. During that time Veda also catered for notable agencies, including the International Women's Organization and CUSO, and for functions at foreign embassies and at Parliament Hill. Along the way she appeared on a number of cooking shows and taught countless cooking classes on Jamaican and African cuisine.

Through her creative flare for cooking, Veda has also contributed to the art of Jamaican cooking. Unofficially, Veda was the first in Canada to prepare and introduce plantain pies, breadfruit stuffing, and Jamaican salted codfish patties.

After more than forty years of professional cooking, Veda has now compiled her food adventures in her first cookbook. Experiencing what has been a delightful culinary journey, she says, "In some ways, I feel I owe a great deal to a forgotten pig!"

Marrett Green

Marrett, Veda's son, has been with Veda every step of the way. Marrett moved with his family to Canada at age six. After seven years helping Veda operate her restaurants, he moved on to study broadcast journalism. From 1992 to 1999, Marrett worked as an award-winning television newscaster at several Canadian stations, culminating as the weekend news anchor at Global Television in Vancouver, British Columbia.

In 1999 Marrett became the Media Relations Officer for the regional government in Greater Vancouver. Marrett is currently working on a children's book for his ever-curious two-year-old sons, who live with him in Vancouver.